NARCISSIST
THE OTHER N-WORD

FROM GASLIGHT TO DAYLIGHT
WITH A COVERT NARCISSIST

DEVYNE BLESSINGS

Caught in the subtle yet devastating grip of a covert narcissist, one woman embarks on a journey of awakening, uncovering the lies, gaslighting, and emotional destruction that nearly broke her. Through raw honesty and hard-won resilience, she learns to reclaim her power, heal her wounds, and rewrite her story. This gripping narrative offers hope, strength, and a roadmap for anyone ready to break free from the shadows of a toxic relationship and embrace the light of self-worth.

Disclaimer:

This book is a work of nonfiction and is based on the author's personal experiences and recollections. In some cases, names, identifying details, and other elements have been changed to protect the privacy and identities of individuals. These changes are not intended to misrepresent any person but to respect their confidentiality.

The events, conversations, and experiences described in this book are presented to the best of the author's memory and may reflect their subjective perspective. Any similarities to actual persons, living or deceased, are purely coincidental and not intended to represent or implicate any specific individual. The author does not intend to harm, defame, or infringe upon the rights or privacy of any individual mentioned or referenced in this work.

The author and publisher disclaim any liability for inaccuracies or omissions and encourage readers to use their discretion when engaging with the content presented.

tox·ic

/ täksik/

very harmful or <u>unpleasant</u> in a <u>pervasive</u> or <u>insidious</u> way.

"a toxic relationship"

FOREWORD

In the pages that follow, readers are invited to embark on an intimate journey into the life of a supply, a woman whose resilience and determination shine through the shadows of a toxic relationship with a covert narcissist. "Narcissist The Other N-Word" is a compelling narrative that unravels the intricacies of psychological manipulation, exploring the silent anguish and eventual triumph of one woman's spirit.

The title might get a lot of different reactions. Like its controversial racial counterpart, The Other N-Word, "narcissist" makes us rethink our views. It comes with a lot of history and triggers strong emotional responses.

The foreword of this narrative dives into the tricky charm that comes with covert narcissists. We look at the early days of her relationship with Ari, where his fake humility hides a web of emotional manipulation. The story reveals the sneaky tactics of the covert narcissist, showing a journey of control, gaslighting, and the gradual breakdown of self-worth.

As we navigate through her emotional landscape, the book explores the impact of the narcissistic dynamic on her identity and emotional well-being. The reader becomes intimately acquainted with the internal struggle as the covert narcissist's calculated actions cast doubt, instill fear, and leave scars on the fabric of her being. The narrative addresses the isolation that often accompanies such toxic relationships, where your reality is distorted, and escape seems like a dream.

This book doesn't dwell on despair, instead, it sets the stage for resilience and transformation. It showcases her inner strength, highlighting the beginnings of self-discovery that emerge from the wreckage of what was thought to be love turned abuse. Readers are invited to witness key moments of awakening as she confronts her emotional chains and embarks on the challenging path toward healing.

The journey is one of self-reflection and the slow but steady reclamation of personal agency. The book acts as a guide, preparing readers for the emotional rollercoaster that accompanies her pursuit of liberation. It prompts reflection on the universal themes of vulnerability, empowerment, and the enduring human spirit. In conclusion, "The Other N-Word" is not just a recounting of one woman's tumultuous relationship but an exploration of the human experience of navigating the intricate dance between love and manipulation, despair, and hope with humor and insight.

This forward extends an invitation to accompany her as she transcends the chains of covert narcissistic abuse, reminding readers that even in the darkest chapters, the journey towards self-rediscovery and healing is a testament to the resilience that resides within us all.

CONTENTS

Introduction 7

Letter to Victims 9

WHEN IT ALL SEEMS PERFECT

01. Narcissist – The Other N-Word.. 13

02. Why Me? Victim Selection and Sourcing Supply.. 25

03. The Honeymoon Lie - Love Bombing.. 37

THE MASK SLIPS

04. Covert Narcissism Unmasked – Unveiling the Facade 49

05. The Cuckoo's Nest - Gaslighting and Manipulation.. 59

WHEN IT ALL FALLS APART

06. Sex as Power - Devaluation as Control 75

07. Creating Chaos – The Triangulation Trifecta 93

08. Mr. Control Freak and Miss Hypervigilant 99

09. Gone, But Not Really – Discarding and Hoovering. 111

10. Trauma Bonds – The Invisible Chains 123

FROM GASLIGHT TO DAYLIGHT

11. Moving On – Let Go, Forgive Yourself First 135

12. Turning the Page - Pain Into Purpose. 145

13. Starting Over – The New Birth 153

Call to Action: Reclaim Your Power 162

About the Author 165

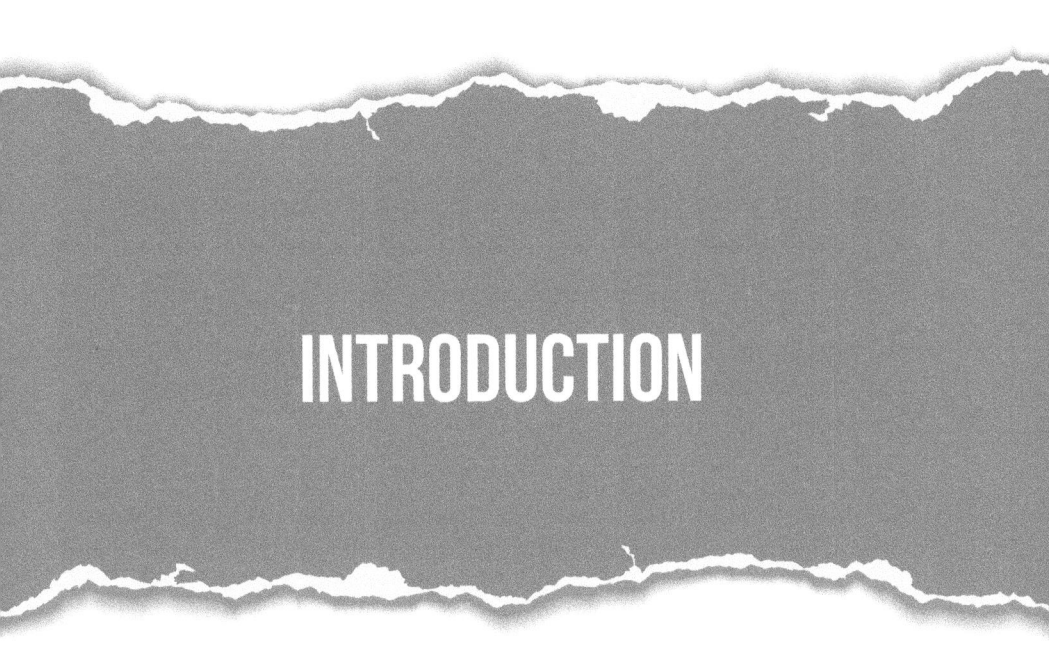

INTRODUCTION

How did someone like me get caught up in such a mess?

Ah, the classic tale of wasting a few cute prime years on a textbook covert narcissist! I thought this alien was my human. You know, handsome, charming, successful, but also, let's be real, a total piece of work. I didn't even know what a narcissist was then, but he sure did redefine it for me!

I wasn't a priority, yet he expected me to fulfill all the roles whenever he pleased. He did the bare minimum but expected maximum effort from me. I spent time questioning my worth around him, feeling like I had to jump through hoops just to earn a smidge of approval. I felt like Charlie Brown when Lucy holds the football and then moves it when he got close enough to kick it to watch him fall. And yes, just like my boy CB, I fell for it multiple times.

After subjecting myself to this dumpster fire of a relationship countless times, I finally mustered the courage to break free (cue dramatic exit music). Trust me, get your popcorn. This book wouldn't even be able to scratch the surface, but I did my best. Although a memoir, I wanted this book to be more of a guide to aid and educate women in recognizing narcissism to avoid a toxic relationship and trauma bonds and how to get the courage to leave.

I decided to wait to write this book until I was close to floating on clouds of gratitude and peace. The last place I wanted to be while writing was knee-deep in the trenches of anger, hurt, and pettiness while pondering how to deliver a healthy dose of revenge. A good, healed, and purposeful head space is the right place to be when sharing intimate details of your traumas and triumphs with the intention of helping others.

When I share my story, the first thing people say is, "I'm so sorry that happened to you." Although I appreciate the empathy, I never viewed my experience through the lens of pain and defeat. The adversity I faced taught me invaluable lessons about resilience, self-worth, and the importance of setting boundaries. These experiences forced me to look inward, understand my strengths and weaknesses, and cultivate a sense of self-compassion and inner strength that I might never have discovered otherwise.

So, while the journey was undeniably tough, I am actually grateful for it. It made me a better person. It showed me what I am capable of enduring and overcoming. It pushed me to grow in ways I never imagined. The pain and challenges were catalysts for my personal development and transformation.

I think it's important to recognize that our most difficult experiences often hold the most potential for growth. When we face our struggles head-on and choose to learn from them, we can emerge stronger, wiser, and more compassionate toward ourselves and others.

So, while I understand and appreciate your sympathy, I hope those can also see why I feel a sense of gratitude for what I went through. It's because of those very challenges that I have become the person I am proud to be with healthy boundaries. Each hardship was a steppingstone on my path to self-discovery and empowerment.

And if I can do it, so can you.

LETTER TO VICTIMS

Dear Victim,

Allow your experience with a toxic person to become an eye-opening journey, one that has taught you invaluable lessons about the kind of person you refuse to be. Understand the importance of setting clear expectations and refusing to settle for anything less than you deserve. No longer will you stay silent and endure, believing that love conquers all. It's time to recognize your worth and prioritize your self-respect and happiness.

You deserve to be heard without ridicule, to receive love without neglect, to be seen and acknowledged, to have undivided attention, and to be respected even in moments of disagreement. Refuse to compromise on these principles. Do not tolerate being oppressed or judged for loving yourself. Embrace your worth and stand firm in your boundaries, knowing you deserve nothing less than love and respect in every aspect of your life.

Never let anyone diminish your essence or silence the voice that liberates your soul. Refuse to settle for those who struggle to embrace your true self, leaving you torn between authenticity and conformity. Don't sacrifice who you are to fit into someone else's mold. Instead, honor yourself, embracing your truth unapologetically and wholeheartedly. You deserve more than begging for the bare minimum only for them to still not deliver.

Toxic individuals resist the journey of self-improvement, choosing to evade facing their true selves out of fear. They rely on excuses, manipulation, and blame-shifting to avoid accountability for their actions. You may have been unfairly blamed for shortcomings you didn't possess and made to feel inadequate while they continuously eroded your self-esteem. Normalize not investing in someone who resorts to anger and manipulation rather than open communication. Withdraw from a relationship where your vision for happiness is disregarded.

Reach a point in your life where empty apologies no longer suffice. They bring about no substantial change. Changed behavior is the best apology, and toxic individuals and narcissists are incapable of this. Repeating the same behaviors without addressing the issues is no longer tolerable. Love, care, and growth necessitate active steps to confront and overcome challenges rather than ignoring or disregarding them.

You have allowed yourself to be devalued, judged, and disrespected under the guise of love, especially when your actions challenged them to be a better man. Stop clinging to someone who takes you for granted, fails to recognize the goodness you bring, offers excuses for unacceptable behavior, engages in petty competition driven by pride and ego, and inflicts intentional pain just to provoke a reaction. You deserve unwavering effort and genuine care, not just when it's convenient for them.

Achieving happiness shouldn't require enduring misery. Both individuals must take ownership of their insecurities and triggers and actively engage in the self-work required to heal past wounds. In toxic relationships, it often feels like you are the only one actively pursuing peace while the other remains burdened and quick to assign blame. Genuine growth demands accountability and dedication to personal development.

You tolerated being soft scolded into him telling you what you lacked and what they needed from you while offering you nothing when you needed and deserved more.

You boosted their ego, supported them through thick and thin, and continued to love them even after being repeatedly mistreated—whether by being dumped, hung up on, ignored, or yelled at. Just imagine the person you could have become had they treated you with the respect you deserved. Surely, you came to this realization long ago, but your emotions and hope that they would change kept you trapped in a cycle of pain, believing that something positive would eventually emerge. Yet, sadly, nothing ever happened.

Adjust your crown, queen. Once you emerge from the darkness, you will realize that you won't see them in the same way. You will change. You will remember your worth. Your lack of optimism will shift. You will prioritize your mental, physical, and emotional well-being. Dark times have a way of revealing true character, and you will begin to see things through a different lens.

Not everyone deserves you. Your fear of conflict, lack of boundaries, and people-pleasing demeanors were deficiencies of self-love. That phase of your life ends now. If you are forced to choose between loving them and loving yourself, you must choose yourself. When a woman leaves a man for herself, she won't be back. You've got this! Go where you are celebrated, one day at a time. I believe in you.

With strength and love,

Devyne Blessings

SECTION

ONE

WHEN IT ALL SEEMS PERFECT

CHAPTER 1:

NARCISSIST — THE OTHER N-WORD

"Every compliment is a hook and every favor is debt."

Life with a narcissist starts with being put on a pedestal. You're their soulmate, their everything, until somehow, you're never quite enough. No matter how much you give, your time, energy, love, even financial support, it's never reciprocated. Instead, they take endlessly, draining you in every way: mentally, emotionally, spiritually, financially. And just when there's nothing left of you to give, they turn the story around. They act as if you've done nothing, as if every sacrifice and effort was meaningless. In the end, they blame you for everything and cast themselves as the victim, leaving you empty and questioning your own reality.

I was on my way to a premiere watch party in the heart of the city, cruising down 85 North as the sun began to set. It was 6 p.m. on a Wednesday, just the perfect time for a solo car concert and some car karaoke. The weather was that warm, 70-degree kind of perfect, and my Cadillac SUV felt like my personal stage. Usher's smooth beats filled the air, and I sang at the top of my lungs, letting the rhythm carry me. I could feel the energy of the night creeping in, knowing I was headed for a quick red-carpet appearance. The sun was giving me a flawless glow that was begging for a car selfie. My long black dress, slit seductively up the side, flowed around me. My hair was parted neatly to the side and tucked behind my ear, with just the right amount of baby hairs perfectly framing my face as I proceeded to Northside Drive with the anticipation of the evening building.

My car concert was interrupted by a call from my good friend Zoe, who, after a few laughs and casual conversation, inquired about the new guy I met. After proudly revealing that I had finally found "the one" just a few months earlier, I found myself in a weird state of confusion, confiding in her over the phone. I vividly remember expressing how I felt trapped in the twilight zone, questioning my own reality. I mentioned to her how every time I brought up an issue with him about us, he had this uncanny ability to twist it around until I was the one left apologizing, even though I had done nothing wrong. I described to her, as I sat at a red traffic light, how, at times, I chose to just deal with it and not confront him because he never took accountability. Any attempts to voice my concerns to him would inevitably escalate into a full-blown argument. I would just rather avoid the confrontation but for the most part, I refused to be silenced. Her response was a blunt affirmation, "Girl, he's a narcissist. I know. I was married to one. You love to research, so why not look it up?"

I told her, "He isn't one of those. He's far from obnoxious, but he can be a slightly subtle manipulating bully."

"There are different kinds, look it up," Zoe said. Little did I know that, at that point, my journey for clarity began.

I've always been a nurturer and healer in my relationships. I'm always looking to see the best in my mate. I never attracted a specific type of man. They all ranged from alpha men to beta men, rich and poor, handsome and basic, 6 pack of abs to dad bods, and everything in between. In 70% of my relationships, I was in more of the dominant role and considered "the prize." That wasn't a position of choice. It was a position via happenstance. I am typically the one who researches, plans and helps execute. The one that didn't ask for much but contributed a great deal. The one where, if he falls short, I can conjure up a plan of success yet never seeking validation but expecting reciprocation. I have always been a woman whose confidence has always been a defining trait in my approach to relationships, with a strong sense of identity and a belief in my own worth.

I grew up in a two-parent home, spoiled, a daddy's girl. My father set the bar, and I learned from him what it looks like for a man to be present, offer affirmation, and show love. He was always present as we hung out like buddies with my friends, and he often gave me cash and credit cards to get whatever I wanted to keep up with the latest fashions and not be deprived of what my friends had. My father was an alpha man and the bread winner. My mother was submissive yet still stern and held her own.

My mother instilled heavily in me the desire to have my own so I wouldn't become dependent on a man for my happiness and livelihood. She raised me to be self-sufficient and independent, to love myself and to never accept or tolerate anything from a man that wouldn't bring me joy and peace.

As a young adult in my 20s and 30s, my confidence became a cornerstone of my professional and personal life. In my career, I pursued ambitious goals, took on leadership roles, and inspired those around me. My professional success, early on, further grew my self-esteem, reinforcing the belief that I deserved fulfillment in all aspects of my life. I've always been a no-nonsense type of woman, unwilling to tolerate any BS and exiting situations quickly that didn't serve me.

In my 20s, getting a man's attention and keeping it was never a challenge. Back then, I had my quirks. I could be possessive, sarcastic, and a little controlling. But gullible or submissive? Never. I always spoke up when something needed to be addressed, making sure my voice was heard in every relationship, respectfully of course. Well mostly respectfully.

Things tended to move fast for me. The first dates often turned into proposals within months, and most of my relationships lasted two to four years. I never stayed in limbo. When one relationship ended, a new one usually began before the seasons could change. Casual encounters weren't my thing. I was loyal to a fault and a true romantic at heart. But I also knew what I wanted, and if my expectations weren't being met, I didn't hesitate to walk away.

One of my more notable chapters was a marriage that began after a whirlwind 30-day courtship. It lasted a several years before I found myself worn down from being the household's sole financial provider. Turns out, love isn't so romantic when it comes with a side of unpaid bills. Live, learn, and add another chapter to the story! That experience taught me a lot about love, partnership, and the strength it takes to say, "Enough."

In retrospect, I don't know how they all deemed me as the one that got away in my 20's because I was more than a handful in my early years, but they do say men love bitches.

As a more mature adult, when I hit my late 30s, I had come to enjoy my space, being single, and not rush into things quickly just for the sake of having someone. By then, I had already experienced being a mother and wife, so there was never a sense of urgency to start over. I also learned patience, compromise, and maturity in relationships, traits I lacked in my 20s and early 30s.

When I hit my 40's, dating became challenging. Most of the men who approached me were in their 20s and ages I wouldn't consider anything serious with. I didn't desire boy toys but seasoned men. The 40's is the age where men were either coming up out of a divorce and needed to heal and live their best single lives or looking to retire from the streets and have babies. Finding someone healed, established, and not desiring children was difficult, so if you did meet someone who checks those boxes, you find yourself wanting to take the time to invest in them.

The other N-word, the term "narcissist," is one we've all heard, overused, and even thrown around casually. Yet, its true meaning often escapes us. I used to associate it with loud, aggressive individuals, the kind you'd expect to be bullies or just plain jerks. Little did I realize there's a whole spectrum of narcissistic behavior, and it's not just about being mean or arrogant. It's a complex disorder. One that I had no idea of or completely understood until recently. Delving into the topic revealed layers I never knew existed. What's truly astonishing is that narcissists often fail to recognize the harm they inflict and instead see themselves as victims. They will act like the victim in a problem they created. They will stab you in the chest and get mad at you because you bled on them. They are creatures that thrive in chaos because chaos brings them peace, and it's a reality that runs deeper than I ever imagined.

The term "narcissist" originates from Greek mythology, where Narcissus was infamously enamored with his own reflection. In psychology, narcissism signifies a personality trait characterized by grandiosity, an insatiable need for admiration, and a lack of empathy and accountability. However, its usage in pop culture and everyday language often strays from its clinical definition. Many employ it casually, attributing it to anyone perceived as self-centered without a comprehensive understanding of its effects.

Confusion often arises between confidence and narcissism. While confidence can coexist with narcissistic tendencies, not all confident individuals exhibit narcissistic behavior. Yet, the line between the two is frequently blurred, leading to misdiagnosis or oversimplified characterizations. Additionally, the term is sometimes weaponized in relational conflicts, serving as a scapegoat or a tool for shifting blame. This misuse takes away from its real meaning, making it harder to understand and support people who have narcissistic personality disorder.

The widespread presence of the word "narcissist" in mainstream media, podcasts, and everyday conversation worsens its overuse. Its frequent appearance in pop culture perpetuates delusions, further distancing it from its clinical roots and making it more difficult to really understand what it's all about. It's an illness. They are sick people. So as a result, people with real narcissistic personality disorder might not get the help they need, and others might not recognize the signs when someone with this disorder is mistreating them. It's like watering down the meaning of the word, and that's not good for anyone.

While "narcissist" is a useful word in psychology, using it too much in everyday talk distorts reality. It's important to know the difference between someone who's just a bit self-centered and someone who really needs help. Understanding this better can make it easier for people who need support to get it and help everyone understand mental health better. I aim to do that here.

Let's dive further into it. Narcissistic Personality Disorder (NPD) encompasses a spectrum of behaviors, and while there are common traits among narcissists, they can manifest in different ways. There are several different types of narcissists. The most common are covert or overt. My personal experience was with a covert narcissist.

Covert narcissists often present themselves as reserved so much so that you would never assume this person is one. They may portray themselves as humble or modest, hiding their narcissistic tendencies behind a facade of vulnerability, whereas to the public, they appear as model citizens, making it very difficult to believe they are what you say they are. They move more subtly, whereas other narcissists are more overt.

A covert narcissist is the most dangerous narcissist there is due to their narcissism not being overly obvious and grandiose, which allows them to fly under the radar. It can be several years before you even realize you're being abused. By the time you realize it, the damage has been done. They are predators and energy vampires that will suck the good energy from you.

Their sense of superiority is sneaky and passive aggressive. A covert narcissist shows narcissistic traits but in a more subtle way than the classic, overt narcissist. This makes them especially dangerous because you won't see it coming. They often come across as charming, reserved, and even humble, which is very different from the overt narcissist. They're pathological liars and cheaters who lack empathy and have a constant need for praise, admiration, and attention. My nex (narcissistic ex) was a true textbook narcissist who checked off all the boxes.

They're masters of sneakiness. Instead of boldly claiming their superiority, covert narcissists prefer a more subtle approach. Picture this: they'll throw a snide remark your way or poke at your insecurities, then brush it off with a "Can't you take a joke?" They operate under the radar, always striving to prove they're a cut above the rest by constantly comparing themselves to others. These folks thrive on validation and praise. They practically need their ego polished daily. But here's the kicker: when others succeed, it's like a punch to their self-esteem. They might ghost your calls or stand you up just to make you feel insignificant, secretly reveling in your frustration while they sip on their satisfaction.

How would you know if you were dealing with a covert narcissist? There are certain traits that are consistent.

While they may not seek attention overtly, they like to use subtle manipulation to control others. This would involve playing mind games, gaslighting, or using guilt to influence those around them. They use tactics to intentionally distort your reality.

The narcissist struggles with genuine feelings of empathy. They find it difficult to understand or validate the feelings of others because their primary focus is on their own needs and desires. They know how to put on a good front and cry crocodile tears, but it's not real. Their lack of empathy causes them to have difficulty in maintaining long-lasting, healthy relationships. If they are in a long-lasting relationship, it's due to their partner being willing to overlook, accept, and tolerate their behavior. Emotional unavailability and emotional immaturity will create a toxic environment. They know how to sweet talk you and gas your head up to place you on cloud 9, only to happily enjoy watching you fall back to the ground without a parachute.

Gaslighting is a method they use to manipulate and control their partners. It's a form of psychological manipulation that causes their victims to question their own thoughts, memories, and perceptions. They will say things like, "You keep assuming," "That didn't happen," "You have a wild imagination," and "You love to twist things." Hands down it is the most sinister manipulation tactic with the intention of distorting your sense of reality. It will destroy your ability to trust yourself and, at some point, question your own sanity. I will discuss this further in a later chapter.

They will misrepresent your feelings by taking your differing opinions, real emotions, and your past encounters, and flip it to turn them into character flaws to present evidence of irrationality. They will paint and reframe what you are saying to make your thoughts sound ridiculous. This will enable them to nullify your right to have your own thoughts and emotions about their behavior and instill a sense of guilt when you try to establish healthy boundaries. They will put words in your mouth and then portray you as having intentions you don't possess.

The narc will seldom hold themselves accountable. One method they will do is change the conversation to benefit them. In mid-conversation, while you are expressing yourself, they will point out a mistake you made months or even years ago to flip the conversation on you and have you scratching your head about how you ended up there.

A narcissist gauges your character based on your reaction to their mistreatment. If you defend yourself, they see you as abusive. If you emulate their behavior, you're labeled vindictive. If you call out their actions, you're deemed petty and immature. Ultimately, they seek unquestioning acceptance, expecting you to say and do as they please without resistance. They blame you for any conflict if your response doesn't meet their demands. You're a hamster in a wheel never reaching your destination. You can't win.

They will never offer constructive criticism, but they will offer destructive criticism and find faults to where it feels like a personal attack. Their intention is never to help you but to nitpick and break you down. They are professionals at moving the goalpost to ensure they will have plenty of reasons for you to be dissatisfied with yourself. They will criticize how you wear your hair, the clothing you choose to wear, your body shape, or weight. The goal is to create a sense of unworthiness to where you never feel like you're enough. They will zoom in on something that they don't like or you did wrong to have you obsessing over said flaws with the intention to emotionally break you. They also know how to do the minimum for you to make it look like they are indeed contributing.

You will bend over backward to fulfill their needs and address their criticism, but it won't change how they treat you. They love to start random disagreements. They will rehash something irrelevant to force an apology or make you prove yourself repeatedly to make you feel unworthy and deficient and you will live in a continuous state of perpetual turbulence.

Narcissism does not just exist in intimate relationships but also in friendships and family dynamics. A narcissist who is a significant other could also be a sibling, a friend, and a parent. A parent with narcissistic traits may prioritize their own needs and desires over those of their children. They might use their children as extensions of themselves, seeking validation and admiration through their child's achievements or appearances. This can result in emotional neglect, as the parent may lack empathy for their children's feelings and experiences. However, in public and on social media, they will intentionally present themselves to be the model parent, and the humble, kind, positive thinking individual creating a facade that doesn't exist. Their social media accounts are carefully and strategically crafted to present them how they want to be perceived.

Growing up in a narcissistic family environment can have profound effects on the narc's children's self-esteem and mental health. They may internalize the narcissistic parents' criticisms and develop a distorted sense of self-worth. Additionally, children may struggle with forming healthy relationships and boundaries in adulthood.

When the narc is a sibling, they may seek to dominate or undermine others to maintain their sense of superiority. They will seek to be the leader of the family, even over the parents. This will create a toxic environment of rivalry and jealousy within the family. Other family members may enable the narcissist's behavior by accommodating their demands or overlooking their mistreatment of others. This can perpetuate the cycle of narcissistic abuse and prevent healthy boundaries from being established within the family unit. Family members may develop codependent relationships with the narcissist, feeling responsible for meeting their emotional needs and sacrificing their own well-being in the process. This can lead to feelings of guilt, anxiety, and low self-esteem.

Overall, narcissism within family members can create a dysfunctional dynamic characterized by manipulation, competition, and emotional abuse. Recognizing these patterns is the first step towards establishing boundaries, seeking support, and fostering healthier relationships within the family unit. If you suspect you're with a narcissist, it is more than likely there will be some beef between them and family members.

Narcissists also love to deliver smear campaigns on their supply to those who have failed them, left them, or cut off supply to them. Their smear campaign is like a toxic PR blitz aimed at tarnishing your reputation. It's when they spread lies, rumors, or half-truths about you to others, painting you as the villain while portraying themselves as the victim or hero. It's a calculated effort to discredit you, isolate you from support networks, and manipulate others into siding with them.

Flying monkeys are the narcissist's foot soldiers, people they manipulate into taking their side, spreading lies, and doing their will. When my narcissist and I fell out, he immediately went on a mission, reaching out to my inner circle, hoping to turn them against me. He spun his web of lies, played the victim, and tried to recruit them into his smear campaign. But there was one major flaw in his plan, my people know me. They saw right through his manipulation and refused to entertain his nonsense. Instead of gaining allies, he exposed himself. His desperate attempts to tarnish my name only backfired, leaving him looking unhinged and untrustworthy. In the end, all he did was isolate himself while I stood firm, surrounded by people who remained loyal to the truth.

It's crucial not to dismiss the warning signs or rationalize their behavior. Despite their apparent humility, covert narcissists are experts at deflecting blame and avoiding responsibility for their actions. There is absolutely zero accountability taken. In the rare instance they do, it's a ploy to earn your trust, but it is not genuine. They may appear sympathetic on the surface, but a distinct lack of genuine empathy lies beneath the mask.

I remember reading something online that said, "a narcissist wants the authority of a king but the accountability of a toddler." I felt that when I read it. They also lack the necessary empathy and cognitive reasoning to resolve conflict.

In relationships with them, it's essential to remain vigilant and trust your instincts. Don't ignore the red flags or make excuses for their behavior. Recognizing that their inability to be accountable and demonstrate true empathy is a fundamental aspect of their personality, and attempting to change them is often ineffective and a pipe dream. You will be selling yourself wolf tickets.

CHAPTER 2:
WHY ME? VICTIM SELECTION AND SOURCING SUPPLY

*"He didn't choose me because I'm weak.
He chose me because I was strong."*

Narcissists stay with those who confront them the least and tolerate them the most. They don't stay because you're "the one" they stay because you are "the one" they can easily manipulate.

They have a constant need for external validation and affirmation of their self-worth. This need is often insatiable, and they may seek "narcissistic supply" to maintain their inflated sense of self-importance. In the context of dealing with a narcissist, the term "supply" refers to the attention, admiration, validation, or other forms of emotional support and acknowledgment that a narcissist seeks from others. The supply is also referred to as the individual providing it.

Narcissistic supply is like a buffet for the narcissist. It's their all-you-can-eat feast of validation and attention. It's their version of a vampire's blood bank, their lifeline to feeling powerful and important. It is their oxygen and the air they breathe. They will feed off negative supply and positive supply.

Negative supply from a narcissist is the toxic energy they feed on when they create drama, provoke arguments, or cause emotional pain. Your tears will give them an ego boost. They thrive on the chaos and emotional reactions they elicit from others, gaining satisfaction from your distress and confusion. This negative supply reinforces their sense of power and control, making them feel superior and significant. They deliberately stir up trouble and manipulate situations to keep you off balance, ensuring they remain the center of attention and continue to extract this destructive energy from you.

Positive supply refers to any form of attention, admiration, or validation that reinforces the narcissist's sense of self-worth and superiority. This could include compliments, praise, or admiration from you or others. Telling them "Thank you," telling them they're right and you're wrong, or you are allowing them to avoid accountability are examples of positive supply. In a toxic relationship, the narcissistic partner may initially shower you with love, affection, and attention (known as love bombing) to gain your trust and admiration. However, this behavior is often conditional and manipulative, serving to control and exploit you emotionally.

You may feel compelled to constantly seek the narcissist's approval and validation, leading to a cycle of dependence and insecurity. You may suppress your own needs and desires in favor of appeasing your narcissistic partner, further reinforcing the power dynamic.

Overall, in a toxic relationship, the back-and-forth between negative supply and positive supply serves to maintain the imbalance of power and control, with the narcissistic partner manipulating you to meet their own emotional needs. Breaking free from this dynamic often requires recognizing the manipulation tactics at play and seeking support to establish healthy boundaries and regain your independence. The issue is that the manipulation isn't recognized until you're in too deep.

They carefully select their partners based on who can serve up the juiciest supply, but when the gravy train stops, watch out! They'll hunt for new sources of supply. They thrive on admiration and compliments, soaking up every ounce of positive feedback like a sponge. They demand constant attention, craving the spotlight in every conversation and event. After all, in their world, it's all about them and not you, all the time. They will do it so subtly that you wouldn't even notice.

Since they require constant validation of their thoughts, opinions, and actions, they may become upset if you don't agree with them or if they receive any form of criticism. An ideal supply to a covert narcissist is one who doesn't challenge them and one that lets them feel they're right all the time, no matter how wrong they may be. Those are the ones that play themselves, have the deepest trauma bonds, and stick around the longest. Those are the ones the narc will have the longest encounters with and even marry.

Narcissists can also self-supply and receive it from controlling or dominating others. They feel a sense of power and superiority when they can manipulate or influence those around them. Another excellent source of supply for them is someone who isn't mindful of their manipulation. Creating drama or manipulating situations can be a way for narcissists to garner attention and emotional reactions from others, providing them with a form of supply.

The nostalgia you feel with a narcissist is a façade because narcs possess a reduced amount of empathy, especially when it comes to recognizing and responding to the emotions of others, which is why they lack conflict resolution skills. Narcissists struggle to see things from other people's points of view. They are so focused on their own needs, desires, and perspectives that they have difficulty comprehending or acknowledging the feelings and experiences of those around them.

You might feel like you've hit the jackpot in love, with someone ready to take a bullet for you, but don't be fooled: they're too busy admiring their own reflection to truly connect with anyone else's emotions. Their charm is like a shiny distraction, blinding you to their true self-absorption. Sure, they can shed a tear or two, but don't mistake it for genuine empathy or care, it's just another weapon in their emotional manipulation arsenal. Their responses are all about them and their agenda, with little room for anyone else's feelings. And trust me, there's always an agenda lurking beneath the surface. So don't expect a shoulder to cry on when times get tough unless, of course, it somehow benefits them. They will appear helpful and sympathetic on the outside, but on the inside, it's a tally mark on the scoresheet they are keeping. They would love to have you owe them.

They will use their understanding of others' emotions not to empathize or provide support but rather to control and manipulate. They may exploit vulnerabilities, emotional needs, or insecurities in others to achieve their own goals. Narcissists can be charming and charismatic, but this appeal may be more about self-presentation than a sincere interest in others. They may use good looks, good sex, and charm to manipulate or control situations rather than to establish authentic connections, making it very easy to abuse and walk away.

Individuals who lack empathy often have an inflated sense of entitlement, believing that their needs and desires should take precedence over others. This attitude leads to a lack of understanding of the feelings and needs of those around them. The only way they will like you is if you compliment their image, and they're able to control you. Other than that, you're deemed a non-factor, but they will continue to keep you around so long as you're providing them with the supply and attention they need. The more supply you give them, the longer they intend on keeping you around, making it harder to leave when you're ready.

One type of person narcissists prey on and are highly attracted to is highly sensitive people and empaths. These are the types of individuals they feel they can easily manipulate and control. Empaths tend to provide a lot of love, compassion, and support. They don't see it that way or appreciate it. They see it as a weakness. That sucks right? Imagine pouring into a person who has no intention of pouring back. Empaths tend to accept the blame and internalize their feelings, making them an excellent supply for the narcissist.

I've always been gifted with a sixth sense for people's emotions, highly intuitive, empathetic, and, dare I say, a professional "feeler." Maybe it's because I'm a Cancer, and as every horoscope ever written will tell you, we wear our hearts on our sleeves, until of course, someone crosses us. Before I discovered the magic of boundaries, I was like an emotional bartender, pouring into everyone I loved while my own cup sat bone-dry.

If you're wondering what an empath is, let me give you the rundown. Empaths are those rare unicorns who can feel and understand other people's emotions with an almost supernatural clarity. We're practically walking emotional Wi-Fi routers, picking up on everyone's energy, moods, and vibes. Here's the kicker: this gift doesn't just let us recognize feelings, it often makes us absorb and internalize them like emotional sponges.

This heightened sensitivity makes empaths especially vulnerable to one specific personality type: the narcissist. The dynamic between these two is often a toxic, co-dependent dance that's as magnetic as it is messy. Why are we so drawn to each other? Why does it feel impossible to break the connection? The dynamic between narcissists and empaths is often described as a toxic and co-dependent relationship, and several factors contribute to the attraction between the two. Let's examine how and why this bond can be so strong.

The insatiable desire for admiration and validation is a prominent trait among narcissists. Empaths, characterized by their caring and nurturing qualities, may inadvertently meet this need by offering the continuous attention and affirmation that narcissists incessantly seek. Empaths are also known for their deep compassion, understanding, and ability to connect with the emotions of others. This compassionate nature can be appealing to narcissists, who may be drawn to the empathy and attention they receive from empaths.

Narcissists often seek control and power in relationships. Empaths, with their nurturing and accommodating nature, may be more prone to tolerating and adapting to the narcissist's manipulative behaviors, allowing the narcissist to maintain a sense of control. Once you adapt to their level of manipulation, it is very easy to find fault in yourself from their accusations. Let me repeat that. Once you adapt to their level of manipulation, it is very easy to find fault in yourself from their accusations.

Empaths are often generous with their time, energy, and emotions. They may be willing to give and sacrifice for the well-being of others, even to their own detriment. Narcissists, seeking to exploit this generosity, may take advantage of the empath's willingness to provide care and support. They may have a high tolerance for emotional turmoil and a strong desire to fix, help, or heal others. Narcissists, with their own emotional issues and instability, may be drawn to empaths who seem capable of navigating and soothing their emotional storms.

In the early stages of the relationship, the empath's selflessness and the narcissist's self-centeredness may create a seemingly complementary dynamic. The empath's desire to give may align with the narcissist's desire to receive, creating an initial sense of balance, a yin to the yang.

It's important to note that while the initial attraction may appear mutual, the relationship between a narcissist and an empath is often unhealthy and damaging for the empath. The narcissist's manipulative tendencies and lack of genuine empathy can lead to emotional, psychological, and sometimes even physical harm for the empath. Recognizing these dynamics and establishing healthy boundaries becomes crucial for empaths to protect their well-being and avoid falling prey to the manipulative tactics of the narc. In relationships with narcissists, an empath's desire to heal and fix can become a dangerous trap, leaving you emotionally exhausted and unfulfilled.

Narcissists are skilled at presenting a compelling facade, often exuding confidence, charm, and magnetic charisma. Beneath this mask lies deep insecurity and emotional dysfunction, traits that can be invisible at first but emerge slowly as the relationship deepens. To someone with a natural inclination to heal, this hidden vulnerability may ignite a desire to help. You may see their wounded side as an opportunity to love them into wholeness. However, what starts as compassion can quickly turn into a toxic cycle of giving without receiving, trying to repair someone who does not believe they are broken.

This attraction often stems from unmet emotional needs in your own life. Perhaps you learned early on that love must be earned through caretaking, sacrifice, or endless patience. Narcissists exploit this belief, pushing boundaries and testing limits while keeping you tied to the hope that your love can transform them. But the truth is, narcissists don't seek to be healed, they seek control, validation, and admiration. Your healing efforts only feed their ego, while your needs are ignored or dismissed.

Narcs choose their victims/supply carefully and strategically. You are not a love interest. You're a target. If the narc feels you are unable to be manipulated and controlled, then you are of no use to him. Remember, they need that supply.

They cannot and will not be alone. They will always have a main supply and a backup supply. They gravitate towards individuals they can groom and upgrade their appearance to take credit for "I made you." They are also keen on how they are perceived by others. They love looking like the man amongst their peers, so who they choose will either be the average-looking one who is willing to upgrade, drop dead beautiful, or highly successful. Both traits would be a plus, but the one with the average looks would overcompensate with her success, whereas the less successful would overcompensate with looks.

Although narcs like to get their best supply from empathic individuals, they also love to target independent, strong, and successful women. Women who are business owners, influential, and financially secure. They love this type because it is much more fulfilling to take someone strong down rather than take down someone already weak or vulnerable. The idea of being able to control and manipulate a person who is accomplished, confident and self-assured can be appealing to narcissists who seek power and dominance. They love to prey on those that are strong enough to compete with them yet weak enough to admire them.

Narcissists are concerned with maintaining a positive image and seeking validation from others. Being in a relationship with a successful and strong woman can contribute to the narcissist's perceived status and enhance their self-esteem by association. Your strength is of great value to them. They would brag about their supply's success or beauty, whichever stood out more. An attraction would be strong and successful individuals who often have access to resources, both financial and social. They love women in power positions, women with money or influence, popularity, or business owners. Narcissists may be attracted to these resources and view a relationship with a successful woman as a means of gaining access to a comfortable lifestyle or influential social connections.

They are drawn to qualities they lack, and they may see strong and successful traits as desirable and convenient because it makes it easier for them to get away with not providing and makes it easier for their behavior of doing the bare minimum to get overlooked. They could also easily get away with doing the bare minimum because their supply is independent and well-established. Yet, they will make miniscule investments knowing the end game is a payout and control.

Initially, the narcissist may genuinely admire the strength and success of the individual. However, as the relationship progresses, this admiration can transform into envy or resentment, leading to manipulative behaviors aimed at diminishing the partner's accomplishments. It's crucial to understand that these dynamics can be harmful to the strong and successful woman involved. Strong and successful individuals may become targets for narcissists seeking to exploit their qualities for personal gain. Recognizing these patterns early and establishing healthy boundaries becomes essential for the well-being of the person involved in such a relationship. If you wear your heart on your sleeve AND are successful, Bless your heart, you're an ideal candidate for a narc's supply and he will do everything in his power to keep you around in his life, even after he discards you. He will never let you go unless you cut off his access.

He rarely supported my business endeavors. The only time he did was when we were on bad terms and he wanted to get back into my good graces, if there was a benefit in it for him somehow, or to use that support as leverage to be able to add it to his list of things he'd done to later throw it back in my face.

One thing about narcissists is that they prefer multiple sources of supply. They have a constant need for attention. You will never be the only person on their mind. They will constantly be preoccupied with finding their next prey, even while declaring you are the love of their life when you are nothing. THEY WILL NEVER BE OF SERVICE TO YOU IN ANY CAPACITY BUT WILL ALWAYS EXPECT TO BE SERVED. YOU WILL BE VIEWED AND JUDGED BASED ON HOW YOU SERVE THEM.

With all of that said, a narcissist wouldn't deny a weak individual. The weak individuals they play with and have sex with, yet the stronger individuals with big hearts are the ones they solidify make-believe relationships with.

One crucial point to bear in mind is that covert narcissists seldom struggle to find a source of validation and another romantic interest because they tend to be smooth and charismatic. You'll observe that they often have numerous partners, some of whom they maintain long-term relationships with. For instance, my narcissistic partner was married for over 20 plus years. Her staying for over 20 years isn't an indication he isn't a narcissist, but it's an indication of how good a manipulator he is. It's important to realize that this isn't a challenge for them. Just understand that their new partner is being manipulated in the same way you were, and their ex was. The new supply is either naïve to it or tolerant of it.

"Which dress did you decide on?" My friend asked.

"The one that doesn't show too much. I responded.

"Well, hopefully, it's a garbage bag." She chuckled.

Every year, we debate about what type of dress we will wear. We attend an annual event in Atlanta hosted by a fraternity.

Every year, there are men galore, dressed to the nines, and the women wear sundresses. We eat, dance, and mingle outdoors for several hours.

It was a long, hot day of fun, food and music. While we were on the verge of leaving, my friends left while I searched for a restroom. Navigating through thousands of people, I spotted a tall, handsome, muscular man over 6 feet with a bald head and goatee. He was wearing gray pinstripe slacks and a gray vest and a gray hat. He had on a fitted pink button-up short-sleeved shirt that accented his physique. His bald head was glistening with sweat, and I was totally prepared to lick, I mean wipe it off.

I adjusted my breasts so they could look perky and mapped my path to cross his, my heart pounding with each step. I wasn't looking directly at him, at least not yet, but I was hyperaware of his presence. My goal was simple, to get close enough to catch his attention, to leave just enough of an impression that he couldn't resist making the first move.

As I approached, our eyes locked. It was just a brief moment, but it was enough for him to know it was okay to pull up. His smile came slow, deliberate, and his dimples made it entirely too perfect. I couldn't help but return that energy with this coy puppy dog look I do that can send the most masculine man in a tailspin. It felt like an unspoken understanding had passed between us in that instant, something neither of us could explain but both knew was there.

I walked past him, hoping he'd take the bait, my heart racing like I was back in high school hoping my new crush would notice me. And then, just as I began to doubt myself, I felt a light tap on my shoulder.

I turned, and there he was, standing even closer than I'd anticipated. His presence was commanding, his frame towering over me, and while his shirt clung to him from the day's heat, it only added to his appeal. Yes, he was sweaty—*very* sweaty—but somehow, he still managed to smell amazing, this mix of clean and masculine that made my thoughts go places they shouldn't. Out of nowhere my private area had a heartbeat.

"Hey," he said, his voice deep and smooth, the kind of tone that could make a woman forget her own name. He smiled again, and I swear the world blurred around us.

We started talking, or rather, *he* started talking. Words spilled from his lips about how he recognized me, how he'd seen me before. I nodded, pretending to follow along, but the truth? I didn't hear a single thing he said. I was too distracted by the way his lips moved, the warmth in his smile, the sheer *presence* of him.

All I could think was, *damn, he's fine.* My brain refused to hold onto his words, and all I could do was stand there, captivated, hoping I looked more composed than I felt.

I studied his moist, full lips moving and heard nothing he was saying. I played it cool and didn't let on how smitten I was. We laughed and chatted for around an hour. The urge to go to the restroom was gone. Feeling a connection, I mentioned my departure, and he offered to accompany me to my car. Politely declining the offer, I suggested exchanging contact information for further discussions. To maintain discretion, he assured me he'd privately message his phone number to my social media inbox. I told him he didn't even know my social media handle.

He replied, "I know exactly who you are." Smiling and accentuating his dimples. "You're my internet crush. By the way, my name is Ari."

He did not want to be seen pulling out his phone and putting my number in it because he probably received several that day. In retrospect, that should have been a red flag. However, true to his word, he messaged me, and that night, we talked for hours until 3:00 AM.

Our daily conversations continued seamlessly, with him even Face Timing me from his bed, sharing moments falling asleep on the phone. The routine extended to the next morning, as he Face Timed me from the shower. Watching the soapy water drip down his muscular back had me moist as one of those rotisserie chickens spinning in the oven at the grocery store.

Excitement filled me as the potential for something meaningful grew. On paper, he seemed to check all the boxes—tall, handsome, charismatic, humorous, successful in a career approaching retirement, a seemingly good father, attentive, caring, sweet, and speaking highly of his faith in God. He even told me he used to be very active and an usher in his church, a church I also once attended.

We talked about everything under the sun. The conversation was enlightening and refreshing. He mentioned he didn't expect me to be as down to earth as I was. We flirted via text when we weren't on the phone and sent unsolicited photos and videos of each other constantly to let the other know they were in our thoughts. We discussed how much we had in common. We attended the same church and liked the same foods. He was avid about fitness, and I was avid about getting into fitness. The conversation remained clean and classy, and I was very impressed with that. I had no idea things would take a turn.

CHAPTER 3:
THE HONEYMOON LIE – LOVE BOMBING

"I was sold a dream and delivered a nightmare."

Love bombing is a trap disguised as a fairytale. In the beginning, he had me picking petals off an imaginary flower, whispering to myself, "he loves me… he loves me not…" Except, in those early days, there was no loves me not. Every petal was a he loves me. No doubts, no second-guessing. Just pure bliss, pure certainty.

I was giddy, floating on air, grinning at my phone like a teenager in awe of her first crush. His texts were poetry, his compliments an endless stream of affirmations. Every word was perfectly crafted to make me feel like I was the one, the missing piece he had been searching for. And oh, did I want to believe it.

It wasn't just the words, though it was the tiny gestures. When he would see me, his eyes lit up like I was the last waffle fry at the bottom of the bag. And trust me, I ate it up. If I casually talked about a song I loved, it was suddenly "our song." He studied me like the last slice of sweet potato pie at Thanksgiving, knowing he wanted it, plotting how to get it, and making sure nobody else grabbed it first.

It was amazing, overwhelming, and downright addictive. One minute, I was an independent woman minding my business, and the next, I was daydreaming about our future together, picking out wedding colors in my head, thinking about what our kids might look like. And the wildest part? He encouraged it. He talked about forever like it was a given. "I just know you're my person," he'd say. And who was I to question fate when it felt this good?

But love bombing is a performance, and the standing ovation never lasts forever. What I didn't realize back then was that the same man who had me believing in soulmates would soon have me second guessing everything I knew to be true. The same man who once had me feeling like the prize eventually had me out here competing, like I had something to prove. But that part? That came later. For now, I was still lost in the fairytale, picking invisible petals, whispering to myself… "he loves me… he loves me… he loves me… "

For now anyway.

Have you ever met someone, and shortly thereafter, there is excessive affection and quick escalation? Not always, but you could be a victim of love bombing. Love bombing is a term used to describe a manipulative tactic in which someone, typically a narcissist, bombards another person with excessive displays of affection, attention, and expressions of love to gain control or influence over them. Their intention is to create a strong emotional bond quickly and overwhelm you with positive attention.

Surface level, it may seem like an outpouring of attention and affection, but love bombing is characterized by its insincerity and manipulative nature. So, although it feels good, it's dangerous and many get sucked into the trap.

Things escalate quickly. They may future fake and embellish the future together, express a deep emotional connection, and make promises early on. The quick pace is intended to create a sense of urgency and commitment even though the feelings they're expressing are not authentic. This is where it all begins.

I began to notice the way he pursued me, which was relentless, calculated, and almost hypnotic in it's purest form. Every morning started with a flurry of texts, his words filled with charm and adoration, as though he had woken up thinking only of me. Throughout the day, my phone would buzz with calls and sweet messages, each one designed to keep me tied to him. Invitations to meet up came with promises of unforgettable moments, and his persistence made me feel like the most desired person in the world. It was overwhelming, yes, but also intoxicating. Who wouldn't be drawn to someone who seemed so captivated, so entirely consumed by the idea of being with you?

At first, I basked in the attention, mistaking his relentless pursuit for passion and devotion. It never crossed my mind that there could be anything wrong with how fast and hard he was moving. After all, isn't this what love was supposed to feel like? The butterflies, the thrill, the sense of being swept off your feet? I told myself I deserved this kind of adoration, that his constant need to be near me was proof of something real and lasting. Red flags didn't exist in my world, not then.

Looking back, I realize how blind I was. The intensity that once felt like romance was something far darker. His every gesture, every call, every carefully worded message was a thread in the web he was weaving, designed not to lift me up but to entangle me. Yet, in those early days, I couldn't see it. I didn't want to. The whirlwind he created was blinding, and I was caught up in its force, unaware that it was slowly pulling me into a storm I wouldn't know how to escape.

Narcissists and love? Like oil and water, they're pros at acting the part, convincing you they care. When they want something from you, it's lights, camera, action. They manipulate folks to secure fallback options because facing their own demons is too scary. No matter how much love you give, they've got a plan B (and C), and they'll keep running the same harmful loops with everyone they meet.

Victims are manipulated by their narcissists. It starts with the idealization phase. At the beginning of the relationship, the narcissist idealizes their target, portraying them as perfect and showering them with an overwhelming amount of attention and affection. They may use flattery, compliments, pet names, and grand gestures to make you feel special and adored. My pet name was Tata Tot, and he called me Tata for short. It sounded goofy but made me blush when I heard it. He knew it too. This phase creates a sense of euphoria and validation for you, which feels as though you have found your soulmate.

As the relationship progresses, the narcissist may work to isolate you from friends, family, and other sources of support. They may discourage outside relationships and activities that do not involve them, monopolizing your time and attention. This isolation serves to deepen your dependence on the narcissist and makes it harder for you to seek help or escape the relationship. My N-word didn't do this. My activities outside of him and time away with friends were an opportunity for him to do what he wanted to do behind my back, so he actually encouraged it.

They rely on manipulation tactics to employ power over you. Tactics like gaslighting, guilt-tripping, and emotional blackmail are all fair game to keep you under their thumb. They will often oscillate between showering you with affection and then withdrawing it, creating a rollercoaster of emotions that would leave you dependent on their approval.

In my own relationship with Ari, this pattern was all too familiar. The constant fluctuations between highs and lows became so normalized that I forgot what a healthy balance felt like, and I celebrated and became overly elated over the highs. I was so caught up in the highs that I failed to recognize they were nothing but minuscule and ordinary. A high would be something so simple as just not having a disagreement that day.

Overall, the process of love bombing is a calculated strategy used by them to secure a source of narcissistic supply. By idealizing, pursuing, mirroring, isolating, and manipulating you, then discarding and hoovering you back, narcissists create an illusion of love and devotion that serves their own selfish needs and desires.

He listened closely to my desires and paid attention to what I wanted and mirrored that. In the early days of our relationship, everything felt like a fairytale. He seemed to understand me on a level that no one else ever had and mentioned to me that no one understood him as I did. It was like he could read my mind, finishing my sentences before I even completed them. He mirrored my interests, my beliefs, my dreams, making me feel like I had finally found my person.

He would have had me anyway, but I made it easier by giving him the roadmap and blueprint. Almost all narcissists love bomb and breadcrumb, and those assholes are so good at it. In the beginning, they seem to adore you and do anything to make you happy. Then, one day, there's a shift in the power dynamic. Although he constantly did the bare minimum and expected me to celebrate it after I was hooked, my narc love bombed me with words a great deal. It was easy to get caught up.

I had plans to go on a trip to Cuba with my close friend. During the planning, I expressed my frustration about not finding a specific hair product. I told him I went to five different locations to find it and finally gave up. In response, he asked for a picture, and within an hour, he located the product, picked it up, and suggested we meet. I was flabbergasted by the effort. We ended up at Target for additional travel items, behaving like a couple shopping for household necessities. We even had the same sneakers on, which were black and white low-top Converse.

In the parking lot, he held me tightly, expressing how much he would miss me and urging me to return quickly. Excited about spending more time together, he dropped a bombshell. He revealed he was legally separated, and his divorce would be final shortly after his daughter graduates High School. My heart sank, and I confronted him, questioning why he hadn't disclosed this earlier. He admitted fearing I would leave him and explained he had already been separated for 4 years and they lived in separate parts of the house. He also revealed he had 2 additional relationships lasting 2 years each during this time of his marriage. That made no difference to me because at that point, I didn't want to partake in that situation any further.

He mentioned that he and his wife had been together since 8th grade and married well over 2 decades. He would constantly talk negatively about her. When I asked him how a marriage that solid could end, his only response was that she talked too loud, she had past childhood issues, and those issues caused them to grow apart. When I asked him to elaborate, he tried and couldn't, but everything pointed to her being the issue, with no accountability on his part. I should have run when he admitted to cheating after I asked him, but I appreciated the honesty instead, now knowing that nugget of honesty was the beginning of a manipulating plan to gain my trust.

Things didn't make sense. He said they went to counseling, and the counselor told him to leave her, but he wanted to wait until their middle child graduated. Something about the story didn't ring true. After a careful investigation of social media accounts, I realized I was being lied to, but I decided to focus on the present despite photos and things showing me something else.

Not wanting to be tied up with his baggage and drama, I wanted to give him a chance to sort things out before considering a deeper and more intimate connection. Life was lifing and I intentionally became engulfed in juggling a corporate job, new opportunities, my real estate career, and starting to visibly engage with someone else. We stayed in touch and built a close friendship although deep down I knew he wanted more, as did I. The timing was not ideal at the moment.

Time passed, and my situation with "someone else" didn't work out due to our crazy schedules and the visibility of our public relationship. I received a call from Ari, the narc, one day asking if he could come over and talk. When he arrived, he informed me that his soon-to-be ex had purchased and closed on a home without telling him and told him she would be moving out in 2 weeks. Immediately, I noticed the red flags because it seemed like the ex was planning an escape from him due to her abrupt departure and keeping her plans from him. He was livid.

Typically, parents would have a discussion, especially when kids are involved. I wondered if she kept it from him because he would try to convince her otherwise or if he would try to derail her plans. At any rate, it did sound an internal alarm with me, but I also saw it as an opportunity as a green light to proceed in getting to know him better. Shortly after, the divorce was final. He would often brag about how he swindled his now ex out of the full equity of the home they owned, and how he made things appear so that he didn't have to give her the bulk of his 401K. It was onward and upward with him, and I was interested in moving forward to see where this was going.

I felt like he held some animosity towards me somehow for not progressing further with him sooner and moving on with someone else, but we both had a lot going on at the time. I am sure he was occupied with others, so I was very cautious in how I moved forward with him.

During this phase, he was the master breadcrumber. He was very successful and well off financially but loved to create an illusion he was broke to avoid doing things a man would typically do for a woman. This is where the low-grade manipulation started.

On paper, Ari was a ten. He checked off all the boxes I required. I inadvertently allowed him to get away with things I wouldn't allow most to get away with. Things progressed rapidly. He was talking about marriage. He would address me in public as "my wife." He even mentioned he would consider a vasectomy reversal if I wanted to have a child. In retrospect, of course, he mentioned this, knowing I had no desire or intention to procreate with him, or anyone for that matter, but it did make me feel good to hear him say this because he stated there is no one he would have ever considered this with.

He loved making grand gestures of commitment. Telling me things like, "I've been a silent admirer of you for a long time." "You're one of the most beautiful women I know." "You understand me more than my ex of over two decades." "I have a list of what my ideal and fantasy woman is and it's you." "I never thought I could love anyone the way I love you." "I'm so addicted to you." "No one can make me feel how you make me feel." "You are my forever." Those were just a few things that I repeatedly heard as things further progressed with us.

He proceeded with showering me with compliments, a few low-budget gifts under $40, unlimited supplies of dick, and declarations of love with the goal of creating a sense of euphoria and attachment to make me more susceptible to his manipulation and exploitation. His love-bombing tactics were not grand, they were minuscule, insincere gestures, but just enough to appear like he was putting forth effort and enough to later throw in my face when convenient.

He continuously praised everything from my intelligence to my sense of style and humor. He would brag about me to his friends while I was in his presence. It was as if he had known me for years, effortlessly anticipating my every thought and desire. Before long, we spent every waking moment together.

Shortly thereafter, I noticed cracks in the facade. His compliments felt rehearsed, his petty gifts seemed more like bribes rather than tokens of affection, and his constant need for validation became suffocating. What I had initially mistaken for love was revealed to be nothing more than a carefully crafted illusion, designed to lure me into his web of lies, cheating, and manipulation.

Inconsistency started and the Jedi mind tricks evolved. Face-up cell phones were now face down. His text responses would be just enough to keep me engaged. Every waking moment decreased to fleeting moments. The love bombing slowed down for no apparent reason whatsoever. I was confused. When he did reach out to me, he could sense my excitement, and it gave him a thrill to know he had me like a yo-yo. He made sure to never be too available or eager to keep me guessing his intentions.

When I mentioned making plans to meet up, He would agree enthusiastically but cancel at the last minute, citing some vague excuse. He could tell I was disappointed, and it seemed to give him an ego boost to let me down.

Despite his inconsistent behavior, I continued to reach out, hoping for more and to get things back to a place of comfort for me. Each time I did, he would respond with just enough attention to keep me on the hook like a flapping fish that got hooked for bait, but never enough to satisfy my longing for assurance and security. It was a delicate balance, but he was skilled at playing the game.

As the days went by, he noticed my messages becoming less frequent and my enthusiasm for him fading. He knew it was a matter of time before I moved on, and at that point, I wasn't pressed, I was good with walking. When he noticed the attention, I initially gave him was starting to decrease, he turned it up several notches. The game switched. The love bombing was bountiful. The phone calls, the constant "I love you," "I need you," "I miss you," "Please don't leave me," "I can't lose you.," Text messages were consistent and abundant, and I found it suspicious. At the point of realization and making the decision to walk away, I was presented with one grand gesture.

"Since we plan to be husband and wife soon, I think it's time you meet my kids. I have never introduced anyone to my kids before." he said.

"Duh, you've been married for over a couple of decades and the women you were involved with during your marriage were in hiding." I thought to myself.

But even still, I was elated to meet those I thought would be my future bonus children. That grand gesture was a major reason for me to overlook his previous transgressions and peculiar behavior.

He set up dinner at a Mexican restaurant. They were two teenagers and a young adult, and they were very pleasant, well-mannered, attractive kids. Dinner went well, and I was eventually able to spend time with them at home, including family nights together. We did family outings together, like bike riding in the park and movie nights. I settled in, and we all became very comfortable around each other.

There was a noticeable lack of effort in the courtship department. Something I would never stand for. Occasions like Mother's Day, Christmas, and Valentine's Day seemed to inconvenience him. His rationale was that after being married for over two decades, he needed to reacquaint himself with the art of courtship. He mentioned to me how the last two women he was involved with during his so-called separation from the marriage didn't demand or expect anything from him and how that was a huge turn-on to him.

He mentioned how he enjoyed the absence of pressure from them because, in his view, his mere presence should suffice. He boasted about how these women didn't expect him to take them on dates or acknowledge them during holidays or Mother's Day and how he found their selflessness pertaining to that attractive. He revealed to me that the women he dates typically are the ones that treat him to dates, gifts, and trips. He even bragged that one of the women he was sexually involved with while married, told him that if he was to get divorced sooner than expected she would give him $1800 a month towards child support and if he allows her to move in his home, she would pay the mortgage. He also bragged about how she purchased thousands of photography equipment for his photography hobby and the large flatscreen TV we watched together but how he wasn't physically attracted to her and wouldn't publicly claim her.

I knew immediately what mind game he was trying to play, but I promptly let him know he had me confused and that is not the norm that I am used to, and I don't roll like that. Although I am a caterer, I will not be the one treating a grown man on dates and trips while he sits back and enjoys the ride and does the minimum for me.

Ari was famous for doing the bare minimum and had an abundance of audacity to keep a tally of those breadcrumbing efforts to throw it in my face when he deemed it necessary. However, I felt in due time, I thought I would hold out that things would change because people could change for the better in the right environment and for the right person. Needless to say, I thought I was the right person. But I was wrong in my assessment. I was sold a dream and delivered a nightmare. My stud was a dud. My Superman was super lame, and my knight in shining armor turned out to be an asshole in aluminum foil.

SECTION
TWO
THE MASK SLIPS

CHAPTER 4:

COVERT NARCISSISM UNMASKED — UNVEILING THE FACADE

"The only changes a narcissist makes is their mask and their victims"

Narcissists often exaggerate their capacity for kindness and empathy. They insist that you should blindly "trust" them without them earning that trust. Initially, they put on an elaborate show of empathy, but as the relationship progresses, their true colors emerge. During the devaluation phase, glimpses of their true, cold, and contemptuous nature become apparent as their false facade begins to show.

The false perception the narcissist creates to onlookers is called the mask. It's the glossy, edited version of themselves that they present to the world, designed to get all the likes and none of the shade. Think of the narcissist's mask as the ultimate Instagram or TikTok filter. It smooths out all the imperfections, adds a touch of glamor, and makes them look like the epitome of perfection. Yet behind that flawless facade lies a whole mess of insecurities, manipulation, and self-absorption. They wear this mask to maintain their image of superiority and to avoid scrutiny or criticism. The mask allows them to blend seamlessly into social situations, appearing confident and charming while hiding their true intentions and calculating behavior. However, over time, cracks may begin to appear in the mask, revealing glimpses of the narcissist's true nature to those who are observant enough to see through the facade. It's essential to recognize that both sides of a narcissist are real, but their kindness is merely a front, a tool for manipulation. The harshness and cruelty you experience reveal the true nature of their disorder.

Narcissists objectify people, focusing solely on their own desires. They treat individuals as tools to fulfill their needs, engaging in transactional interactions. Their struggle to form genuine connections leads them to exploit people as sources of supply rather than foster meaningful relationships. They are also habitual liars but manipulative enough to tell you a truth that is not in their favor to garner your trust. They will use some forms of honesty to disarm you.

A narcissist doesn't truly love anyone. They manipulate people to create safe havens for themselves, always making sure they have a place to go because they're scared of facing and fixing their own problems. The narcissist is a true master of duality. One minute, they're all charm and warmth. The next, they're icy, controlling, and ruthless. This whiplash between personalities stirs up confusion and self-doubt. To the world, they're the flawless Dr. Jekyll—charismatic, generous, the life of every party. Admired by all, they seem like the perfect catch. But once the doors close, out comes Mr. Hyde: manipulative, critical, abusive. The contrast is so jarring it leaves you questioning reality itself. Their public mask is so convincing that friends, family, and everyone around only see Dr. Jekyll, making it almost impossible for them to grasp your experience with Mr. Hyde.

Ari was vile. He didn't care about anything but himself. On the outside, on social media, and the public persona was that of a model citizen, a great dad highlighting his son's sporting accomplishments or his daughters' academic achievements, celebrating his friends and fraternity. But realistically, he was diabolical. He was very good at hiding it and making it obvious to make it easier for you to question yourself and others to question him. He became increasingly manipulative, using tactics such as gaslighting, guilt-tripping, and emotional blackmail to undermine my confidence and my independence. He also resorted to verbal or emotional abuse, criticizing me over the smallest things relentlessly, belittling my accomplishments, and making me feel inadequate and never good enough no matter how good I treated him and catered to him, no matter how often I avoided conflict, and no matter how often I took the licks with closed lips.

As his demands and expectations grew longer than a CVS receipt, conflicts and arguments within our relationship escalated like a high-stakes poker game. Although I knew I deserved the bakery instead of the breadcrumbs, he still did the least yet expected the most. I was struggling with and having an internal tug of war with finding a place of not losing myself and my strength but still trying to accommodate him. I constantly found myself walking on eggshells to avoid triggering his anger or disapproval and stepping on a landmine. Trying to set boundaries or voice my frustrations was like throwing a boomerang. It always came back to hit me with more tension and arguments.

He would often revert to dumpster diving into yesteryear to conjure up something to fuss about, to force me into apology mode or submission. Time went on and he would start arguments as frequently as bi-weekly. The majority of them were petty, a reach, and had no merit. It could have been over anything. I could say, "This chicken is spicy," and he would say, "It's not. It's salty." The minute I disagree, here comes World War III, with something being wrong with my taste buds and palate.

When there was an altercation, he would manipulate and fake the situation to try to make me feel he was making an effort to resolve it. But no matter what, he would try to convince me that I was the bad guy, and he was the victim, even though deep down, I knew it was the other way around. This resulted in me accepting fault for something he did, just to keep the peace.

We would argue over simple things like how I greeted his dogs before greeting him, telling me it made him feel that I loved them more and I was putting him second. He would gaslight me by yelling and giving me the cold shoulder, telling me how wrong I was, how I hurt him when I did it, and how he couldn't see a lifetime with a woman that made him feel like he was second to animals. He would give me the silent treatment and wouldn't speak to me for days. I apologized and started to make it a point, going forward, to ignore the dogs prior to acknowledging him, which was torture because I am a huge dog person. Heck, I prefer animals over humans. Even though I rectified the situation, it continued to become a bone of contention in our relationship when he ran out of things to argue about.

Tuesday night was supposed to be simple with tacos, wings, and a cozy evening at his place. His two dogs, the stars of the household, had other plans. The gray poodle one was shy but curious, while the black one was a bold yet sly little rascal. As I sat at the table, trying to savor a chicken drum, the black one wouldn't let up, his hopeful eyes practically begging me to share. I glanced at him, then at the kitchen, where Ari was busy flipping tortillas. With a quick motion, I held the bone under the table, letting the dog get a taste. I figured a little lick wouldn't hurt. Before I could react, the dog snatched the whole drum right out of my hand and darted off like he'd just stolen a bag of money.

Panicked, I charged after him, grabbing the drum before he could do any real damage. Just as I sat back down, trying to compose myself, Ari turned around. The look on his face made it clear I wasn't as slick as I thought.

"How many times have I told you not to feed the dogs?" he asked, his voice sharp.

"Relax," I said, brushing it off. "I wasn't feeding him. I just let him lick the bone. I got it back immediately."

"That's not the point!" His tone grew colder. "You disobeyed a direct request. Do you even realize you could have killed my dog?"

I blinked, stunned. "Seriously? You're being so over the top. I didn't try to murder your dog!"

"Don't dismiss my feelings!" His voice rose, the veins in his neck becoming more pronounced. "You don't get to decide what matters. Apologize to me. Now."

His intensity caught me off guard. I softened my tone, trying to ease the tension. "Look, I would never hurt your dogs. I'm sorry if it came off that way. It wasn't my intention."

I used my inside voice, trying to diffuse the tension while continuously watching him try to force an apology.

I thought that would be the end of it. I couldn't have been more wrong.

For the rest of the night, he berated me, his words sharp and unrelenting. I felt like a child being scolded, waiting for him to point to a corner and demand I stand there in time-out. And this wasn't a one-off incident. For months after, he brought up that night with the same energy, spinning it into a tale of betrayal and reckless endangerment. Each time, he demanded a fresh apology, as if it had just happened.

But that wasn't the worst of it. The canine craziness was just the beginning, the first taste of how he thrived on control and conflict. His nitpicking became a ritual, slipping into every moment we shared.

One second, we'd be laughing, caught in the joy. The next, his mood would shift, dark and heavy, pulling me into an argument over nothing. His fury felt calculated. His words were designed to cut deeper with every exchange. The light in his eyes turned to darkness, as if chaos fed him, and my confusion and pain were his food.

"Why do we argue so much?" I asked one night, the weight of his accusations bearing down on me. "Why can't we just get it right?"

"It's because I've never loved anyone like this before," he said, his voice trembling with emotion. "You make me feel things I've never felt. I want us to work so badly, but you're so stubborn. You don't listen. That's why I get upset."

I felt myself crumbling under his gaze. To keep the peace, I gave in and said, "I will work on that."

He nodded, his expression softening, though his words still felt like a command. "We need understanding," he said. "You have to let me get through to you."

I reluctantly agreed, not fully grasping what "understanding" meant in his world. But I wanted peace, and in that moment, I was willing to promise anything for it.

Little did I know, "understanding" in his mind was code for control. And I was slowly losing mine.

At the time, I didn't see what he was doing. I slowly started to question myself, but thankfully, my intelligent inner self kept intervening, causing me to question my own self-doubts he was attempting to create. He would ask me to work on myself because he wanted me to be his wife, but I had no idea what I was doing wrong. The truth of the matter is that we argued so much because he knew that I was slowly but surely figuring him out, and it was unhinging him, so he had to increase the manipulation to put me in my docile place, when I have never been in my life been a docile woman.

He started to create conflict out of nothing to keep me feeling off-kilter. He began to thrive on pointless arguments and erupt over minor issues. He then would emotionally withdraw, only to later shower me with affection when he feared losing control of me. His constant Jekyll and Hyde switch between personas left me feeling psychologically unsafe, unsure of who I was going to get each day.

It was one of those chaotic city evenings, the kind where plans unravel and small inconveniences snowball into much larger issues. I'd stopped to grab a quick bite to eat when my car battery decided to give out. Frustrated, I called him, and he swooped in to save the day, bringing along one of his frat brothers. They gave me a jump, recharged my battery, and just as I started to feel relief, he casually mentioned they were heading back to his house and suggested I follow him.

The suburbs we both lived in were familiar, but the city was a different beast, full of construction zones and detours that turned straightforward trips into scavenger hunts. Still, I had his address plugged into my GPS for reassurance. As we rode through the tangled streets, I noticed the next left turn coming up.

I quickly called him.

"Make the next left," I said, keeping my eyes on the road.

"No, you're wrong. Stay straight," he replied, confident.

But I was already in the left-turn lane, boxed in by traffic. "I can't get over. I have to turn left," I said.

There was a brief pause. Then, in an irritated tone, he said, "I don't see you behind me anymore."

"Because I had to turn left," I explained.

His response was brisk. "I'll see you at the house."

Before I could say another word, he hung up. By the time I arrived at his house, I had beaten him there. I waited for them to arrive. I parked and headed inside, trying to shake off the lingering tension from his abrupt goodbye. His two poodles, as usual, greeted me like I was the highlight of their day. The gray one whined, pawing at my leg, waiting for me to scoop him up like I always did. But tonight, I resisted, keeping my distance. I could already sense his agitation, and I didn't want to do anything to set him off further. Still, ignoring those dogs felt like ignoring pieces of my soul.

When he walked in, his frat brother trailing behind him, he avoided eye contact entirely. The energy in the room shifted and turned dark. His frat brother headed to the restroom, leaving us alone for a moment.

"Is something wrong?" I asked tentatively, trying to bridge the gap.

He looked at me, his tone as cold as a disappointed parent. "You know what you did. We'll talk about it later."

I swallowed hard, the words lodging like a stone in my throat. *Here I go again on trial for something I didn't even realize I did wrong.*

While his friend was there, he played the part of the perfect boyfriend—warm, attentive, all smiles. His friend headed to the door and said, "I will leave you two lovebirds to your business."

"No don't leave." I said in my head because I knew all hell was going to break loose. And as soon as his frat brother left, the mask fell away. What followed was a two-hour argument that felt more like a sermon.

"You don't trust me," he said, his voice sharp and deliberate. "You don't let me lead. You don't follow my guidance. Do you know how stupid you made me look in front of my friend by turning left when I told you to go straight?"

I blinked, stunned. "I didn't mean to—"

He cut me off. "It's not just about the turn. It's about what it represents. I need a woman who trusts me to guide her, who follows my lead without hesitation. That's important to me. And tonight, you embarrassed me. I won't tolerate too many more moments like that."

I cursed him out enunciating every syllable. I called him every name in the book. In my head of course and not out loud. The weight of his words hung heavy in the air, pressing down on me like a weighted blanket. It wasn't just about the turn. It never was. It was about control, about power, about him needing me to fall in line or risk his wrath. And as I sat there, rolling my eyes when he wasn't looking, thinking to myself that I no longer liked him as a person, I couldn't shake the sinking feeling that this argument wasn't about us as a couple, it was about him, his ego, and his desperate need to dominate every corner of my world.

"So, if the GPS says you are about to drive off a cliff, and I call you to warn you, and you keep going straight, do you expect me to follow you? I was simply trying to help. I don't see anything wrong with advising you on the right way to go, and it was too late for me to get out of the turning lane," I said.

He avoided my question, unleashed a tirade of yelling and word gymnastics, and accused me of deflecting, all while holding out for an apology like a stubborn toddler refusing to eat their veggies. He would not let up until I apologized for not following behind him. Exhausted and feeling like I'd been through a marathon, I finally caved and apologized, but he still wasn't satisfied.

Like an energy vampire, he drained the life out of me, and I was ready to go home. When I mentioned that I was heading home to get some much-needed rest after a long day, he suddenly urged me to stay the night. Even after explaining my early morning client showings and the dire need for a decent night's sleep, he flipped the script yet again, starting another round of arguments. I told him I couldn't take the risk of oversleeping and that my clients were looking to place an offer on a home, and it was important that I was well rested.

He gave me the silent treatment for two days before reappearing, and I didn't bother reaching out either. He finally called, demanding an apology for "abandoning him when he needed me most," conveniently forgetting his own starring role in the drama. I apologized to keep the peace again, finally realizing this man may not be who I thought he was.

I struggled with finding the error of my ways. I was in the sunken place, trying to find my way above ground. I was living in the matrix. I clung to hope like a fat kid clinging to an ice cream cone in the summertime because, at this stage, it was just cracks in the mask and not the full-blown reveal, but I was starting to question if I was happy here. I was still at the stage of confusion, trying to figure out ways to improve our relationship before it started to spiral while questioning myself if I was part of the problem.

I was at a point of confusion and sought confirmation from a couple of friends. After another conversation with Zoe, who had already led me down the path of researching narcissism, I decided to listen. My first step was to Google, "Is my spouse a narcissist?" A quiz popped up for me to take. Not only did he pass it with a perfect score, but he also got the bonus questions and extra credit, which was not graded on a curve.

To my surprise, I took several of these tests. Some questions were, "Does your partner continuously make you feel like you aren't good enough?" "Does your partner blame you when there is conflict in the relationship?" "Is your partner sensitive to criticism?" "Does your partner have a temper?"

His high test scores prompted me to Amazon, where I ordered books and spent hours watching videos on YouTube, following narcissist social media influencers on TikTok, and listening to multiple audiobooks. It was then that my naivety converted into knowledge. I wish I had just left, but I didn't.

He wasn't just any narcissist, he was the quintessential textbook example of a covert one. I studied his behavior, understood all the manipulation tactics, and delved into the intricate workings of his mind, analyzing every detail and exploring every avenue from A to Z. I spent all my spare time educating myself. I became consumed with figuring out the dynamics. I would frequently book first class tickets on Delta airlines with a final destination to the rabbit hole to try to make sense of his words and actions. My fascination with understanding his behavior shifted from learning if he was a narcissist to finding solutions to either mend his ways or endure his presence. Despite it all, the thought of walking away was not an option at that time.

CHAPTER 5:

THE CUCKOO'S NEST – GASLIGHTING AND MANIPULATION

"They'll create the noise, offer you earplugs, then act as if they've granted you peace and quiet."

For months, things were smooth. No arguments, no sudden discards, just us, vibing. That night, we were on the couch, cracking up at a Kevin Hart Netflix special, tearing into popcorn shrimp and fries. I had my lime water, he sipped on his Old Fashioned. Mid-laugh, he hit pause.

"You know, I still feel like you owe me an apology for your behavior at Home Depot," he said, completely straight-faced.

I double blinked. "What? That was months ago. And if memory serves me, I did apologize. All I did was confirm with the flooring guy that ceramic tile takes longer to install than vinyl, because let's be real, it does. You told me vinyl was harder, so I wanted to be sure."

His jaw tightened. "By questioning me in front of another man! You made me look stupid! And now, instead of just taking accountability, you're arguing with me again. This is the problem with you. You don't respect me. You never have."

"Oh, here we go with this BS" I thought to myself.

"Ari, why can't you let things go?" I sighed. "We discussed this back then. I told you I didn't want to make you feel a certain type of way by asking a specialist. I acknowledged I possibly could have handled the situation differently, and I apologized how my actions made you feel. What I'm NOT going to do is open this up again."

"I'll let it go when you apologize again," he snapped.

"Not happening. I already apologized for how it made you feel, and we moved on."

"Apparently we didn't, because here we are. I don't want you to apologize for making me feel a certain type of way. I want you to apologize for the effed up shit you did!" He was yelling now.

Ten exhausting minutes later, with him still yelling. I caved. "Fine. You win. I apologize. Can we be done with this now? Please just put the show back on."

"If it took all this to get an apology, you can keep it. You don't care about my feelings. You never have! You disregard them over and over!" He whined.

I just stared at him, speechless looking at him like he was crazy. "I just apologized AGAIN. You told me to keep it. And now you're saying I don't care about your feelings?" I asked.

"And every time I try to talk to you about my feelings, you start an argument. I can never get through to you. I can't express myself. How are we supposed to make this work if you refuse to listen and keep picking fights?" He threw his hands up and shook his head like he was the victim and I started it.

At this point, I was sitting there in utter disbelief. This man really just spun an entire one-man production out of nothing, and somehow, I was the villain.

Then came the grand finale.

"Just GO!" He shoved my shoes at me and started gathering my things like I was being evicted.

"I have to set a firm boundary because we need to keep the past in the past!" I said.

"You are my past." He fired back as I was walking towards the door.

"Touche'" I replied with a smirk.

As I watched him unravel, one thought echoed in my head: This N-word has officially lost what's left of his mind. I gladly left the drama, but mad because I didn't hear the rest of Kevin Hart's joke. And like clockwork, the next morning, my phone buzzed. A text. "Hey tata tot".

Like nothing ever happened. Business as usual.

When a narcissist feels threatened because you're setting boundaries, they'll try to alarm you into thinking there will be consequences if you don't agree with them. They want to threaten you into a surrendering state so they can have control over you. They want to groom you over time to become afraid to question, approach, or accuse them. They are systemically envious and will not allow anything to come in between their influence over you. Although it won't outwardly appear this way, they need to always be the center of your world and have full command over you.

You'll never find clarity or get closure when dealing with a narcissist, they thrive on keeping you confused. Even a simple yes-or-no question will elicit a long, convoluted response, leaving you uncertain. They are skilled in their ability to make you doubt your own reality. This is called gaslighting.

Initially, they craft a convincing illusion of a strong relationship, building trust. Then, gradually, they chip away at that foundation. Yet, you grasp onto memories of their earlier loving and trustworthy demeanor, hoping they'll return to it. But that person you idealized never truly existed and never will. They merely mirrored what you wanted to see to draw you in. They studied you, molding themselves into your desired image and convincing you of their authenticity.

We were lying down at my place. I was on my back, staring at the ceiling fan spinning on high. It was spinning so fast that my eyes began to water. The weather was spring, and I remember thinking I heard a woodpecker on the side of the house. I was stuffed because I made shrimp-fried-rice for lunch and homemade egg rolls. It wasn't uncommon for us to lay on the couch or on the bed and have hours of engaging conversation. During this time, he brought up a hypothetical situation. He asked me how I would respond if I randomly saw him speaking to a woman for an extended period of time. I told him that I would watch the body language and, after a while, walk up to them, say hello, and see how he would introduce me.

"Huge turn-off." He responded. "Deal breaker."

"Deal breaker of what?" I asked.

"The woman I prefer in my life and the one that I would marry would not do anything like that. I would expect her to ignore it and not question me about it because that's how a mature, confident, secure, grown woman would handle herself. I find that very sexy and appealing." He said.

I looked at him like he was crazy and chuckled to myself because his reverse psychology and pathetic attempts of grooming and manipulation were now obvious to me.

I simply responded, "Okay. I hear ya." He was attempting to start an argument while trying to gaslight me, and I wasn't up for the challenge. He kept trying to reiterate the importance of this and circling around, but I was able to avoid it like a game of dodgeball.

"I'm going to head home," he stated. "I'm going to go to bed around 8pm in case you call or text, and if I don't answer or respond. I will be sleeping."

Mr. Toxic Dick himself was a night owl and did not go to bed until at least 1 am. I knew ahead of time, after countless hours of educating myself, that his goal was to craft his next masterpiece of manipulation by trying to get in my head to have me stressed and wondering if he was going to be with someone else. I played it cool and decided not to give him the energy he was looking for because I knew it was a set up.

I planned to partake in his antics and call around 9 p.m. to confirm my suspicions, so I didn't give him another thought. When 9:30 came, I called, and of course, he didn't answer. I knew he wouldn't because the whole point was to turn my brain into a swirling mess of doubt and suspicion.

But instead of letting it go and not giving him the pleasure, I succumbed to the urge to prove myself right. I then texted him, letting him know I had called and was thinking of him. I knew one of two things would happen. He would either call me back to quickly finish me, or he would not call until the next day to prolong what he thought would be the agony.

He called me back an hour later, with a fake sleepy voice, yelling at me and accusing me of checking up on him when, all along, I knew he was just setting the stage like a Tyler Perry production to cause a fight.

"You never listen. You disturbed my peace! We just had this conversation earlier. Your actions make me feel like you don't trust me. We need a break from our relationship because I need to re-evaluate our situation. I just can't bring myself to be with a woman who doesn't trust me, so I need some space." He fussed.

I made no accusatory remarks, so him accusing me of not trusting him just reaffirmed the game he was playing.

"Cool, take all the time you need." I said. I played it cool like a boss, but the reality was my stomach was in knots, and I was wondering what his motivation was and if we would get back together. Me, thinking I was outwitting him, did more harm than good and I started to blame myself and realize how toxic this situation was.

His manipulation tactics were elaborate and dramatic, but I managed to stay ahead of the game because by now, I know his tricks. If his plan had succeeded, I would have been stressed out, thinking he was cheating, which could have sent me into a tailspin. But instead, I was on to the games, so my goal was to tough it out until I heard from him. And I knew I would hear from him. He was notorious for orchestrating arguments so he could cheat in peace afterward.

3 days later I received a call from him. I'm not even going to lie. It was a rough 3 days, and I was hoping he would call. When he did, the drama began, and he tried to play the victim.

"Babe, it's a horrible feeling not having the person I love fully trust me. It hurts me so much, especially when I try to do everything right. Perhaps your lack of trust is an issue and may stem from something in your past, or childhood. Either way, I shouldn't have to suffer and pay for it." He whined.

I am sitting there thinking, all I did was call him and text him I am thinking of him. I didn't accuse him, but he accused me of somehow making him suffer and pay. He even told me I needed to seek help for my trust issues. I couldn't believe what I was hearing, but then again, I could. All I could think about is what kind of sick f*ck would orchestrate a scenario to try to hurt me then force an apology from me and mind screw me into thinking it was my problem. He went on to make it a huge ordeal, playing the victim, while I ate my proverbial bag of popcorn to see how the production would play out.

The conversation ended as it always did, with him telling me I owed him an apology and that he was willing to give me another shot at this roller coaster of a relationship, but I would have to do better in the relationship for us to continue and move forward. It was as though humbling myself before him and issuing an apology for something that wasn't my fault was like an intense drug rush to him.

Knowing it was all a set-up, my head was still spinning, wondering what I had done wrong. He was so slick with it that for a minute, I felt grateful for the opportunity, and I even questioned if I was wrong and how maybe it wasn't a ploy. During that period of vulnerability and self-doubt, I apologized to him and even felt guilty for playing a starring role in his production. I even told him that I would make it up to him.

Minutes later, I had a sobering realization that I had just been manipulated, groomed, and played at the same damn time. "Dammit, he got me again." I thought to myself. I also was starting to dislike the fact that he was rubbing off on me for me to voluntarily participate and engage in his narcissistic shenanigans. Trying to outwit him had backfired on me.

The majority of our disagreements arose when I attempted to share my feelings with him on things he has done to make me feel less than. Unfortunately, every time I opened up, he managed to twist the situation, making me feel like I was at fault and leaving me lost in a cloud of confusion. It became apparent that trying to communicate with him was impossible, so I decided to preserve my peace of mind and mental well-being by finding another way to navigate the situation.

He continuously misrepresented my words and portrayed me as having intentions I never had. I was to the point where I wanted to record every conversation because he would continuously tell me I said things I never said. My inner self would tell me to write down what he said and how I was feeling.

There was ongoing nonstop projection. I never had to investigate what he was doing because whatever wrong he was doing he would accuse me of doing it. His intention was to keep me confused, to avoid accountability and avoid addressing the real issue.

Mr. Hurt Hogan would verbally harass me with random phrases and words ready to create the perfect appetizer, a word salad, with a hot buttery side of scorn on the cob. He constantly used meaningless phrases and analogies with the right amount of contradiction to intentionally confuse me. He would garnish it with a sprinkle of lies that would often leave me hungry for clarity.

Here are some of the things he would say to me to project, gaslight, and manipulate me on a regular basis that would cause my head to spin like the exorcist, but it was actually him spewing his word salad to further keep me in the haze, in the matrix, in the sunken place.

"You believe what you think instead of what I tell you. Don't think! Listen!"

"You have a self-righteous way about yourself that makes your assumptions better than someone else's real-life situation. I see it time and time again from you, and it's debilitating."

"Your feelings make my responses to you and my explanations to you resistant to sink in."

"You let your feelings draw your own conclusions and you make a response out of it."

"You draw your own conclusions, and you make a reality out of something false."

"Stop thinking on your own and ask me for an example."

"You embellish the facts that your mind is assuming."

"You don't want to talk and seek clarity to work towards creating understanding in each other."

"You make your own extreme conclusions and reactions by saying the situation is about something that it really is not."

"Your ego keeps getting in the way of receiving anything fruitful."

"You didn't allow yourself to open up and receive things outside of your own thoughts."

"You're letting something stand in the way and it seems it's causing you to evolve in your own world of righteousness over everything."

"You act on your own delusions and not speak from reality."

"You believe what you think and not what I say."

"You've shown me you will never see anything other than what you believe and are not open to trust when it comes to your faults."

"You cover your actions by the reasons of your emotionally charged assumptions which are not reality. Don't assume!"

Do you see what he did there? Ari would speak in cursive and play a verbal game of twister with me anytime I tried to bring up an issue. He continuously aimed to confuse me, making it harder for me to challenge or confront his behavior. His responses were inaccurate and made little sense, yet his delivery was always convincing. He would constantly try to convince me that water wasn't wet and get upset when I corrected him.

Dealing with a covert narcissist is like being trapped in a cheating game of Uno, where they seem to hold all the power cards. The moment you try to hold them accountable, out comes the reverse card, flipping the blame squarely back on you. Just when you think you're regaining some control, they hit you with a wild card, shifting the narrative to something so unexpected that you're left scrambling to keep up and trying to figure out the next color of their mood. And don't forget the skip card, used expertly to dodge any real conversations or responsibilities, leaving you spinning your wheels while they stay comfortably in control.

Toxic individuals are like master illusionists, luring you into a false sense of safety just so they can showcase their malice. You might start with a polite disagreement, but before you know it, you're in the ring with someone who's about as respectful as a bull in a China shop. What began as a civil exchange quickly reveals their true colors. They're not here to play nice, they're here to tear you down.

In the world of narcissism, there's a term that perfectly explains one of their go-to tactics: **DARVO**. It stands for **Deny, Attack, Reverse Victim and Offender**, and it's a manipulation strategy that keeps them in control while leaving you feeling confused and invalidated.

Here's how it plays out. When you call a narcissist out on their behavior, the first thing they'll do is **deny** everything. They might say things like, *"That never happened,"* or *"You're imagining things."* This denial isn't just about avoiding responsibility, it's meant to make you doubt your reality and question what you know to be true.

Once denial is in place, they'll **attack**. Instead of addressing what they've done, they'll turn the focus onto you. *"You're overreacting,"* or *"You're so sensitive, why do you always make a big deal out of nothing?"* They might even accuse you of being the problem, deflecting attention away from their actions. This is designed to put you on the defensive, making you feel like you have to justify your feelings.

The final move is to **reverse the roles of victim and offender**. They'll paint themselves as the real victim, claiming you've wronged them by confronting their behavior. They might say, *"I can't believe you'd think that about me,"* or *"After everything I've done for you, how could you accuse me of this?"* Suddenly, they're the one who's hurt, and you're left feeling guilty for even bringing up the issue. The original problem is completely overshadowed by this role reversal, leaving you emotionally drained and questioning yourself.

DARVO is a calculated way to dodge accountability and manipulate the narrative. It shifts blame, avoids addressing the real issue, and leaves you feeling like the offender for simply standing up for yourself. It's one of the most disorienting and damaging tactics in a toxic relationship.

Recognizing DARVO is crucial. When you see this pattern playing out, remind yourself that their denial doesn't erase the truth, their attacks don't define you, and their role reversal is a distraction, not reality. Standing firm in your perspective is how you start to break free from their control. Remember, you are not the offender for demanding respect, you are reclaiming your voice.

Towards the tail end of the relationship, I was manipulated into thinking that being single with him is better than being in a relationship with him with a title. Here is how he did it. When we didn't have a title, there were very few arguments and little to no devaluing, and he wasn't able to discard me. However, he carried on like we were a couple. Pretty much, I was in a relationship with him, but he wasn't with me. We still spent a considerable amount of time together. Friends would say," I thought you two weren't together anymore. You're always together." I would respond with, "We're just friends," while in my head, knowing I was in a one-sided relationship. He intentionally made things tumultuous when there was a title and free and easy when there wasn't to condition me into being happy single, yet still with him. Unknowingly, I was duped into agreeing to him having his cake and eating it, too, without even realizing it. He kept a strong presence in my life, making it impossible for me to pursue anyone else. After deciding that the arrangement was not for me, I gave him an ultimatum, and he eventually chose to have a title as a couple, but it didn't stop his motion to do what he wanted to do or make it hard for me.

He frequently resorted to fabrications such as, "I heard you cheated on me," or "Someone told me you said/did this," aiming to provoke a reaction. Aware of his tactics to instigate doubt and confusion, I remained composed, refusing to indulge in his manipulative games. Instead of escalating the situation, I would calmly inquire, "Do you believe them?" His explosive reactions to my composed responses revealed his true intentions. He always sought turmoil, not resolution.

Of course, after walking away, I found out about numerous women he was cheating with. Insecure females who knew he was in a relationship with me, who were willing to smile in my face in person and happily play the position of side salad Sally, waiting patiently and desperately to get off of the bench and for the coach to put them in the game. They were passengers on his bus willing to ride endlessly on it.

The entire time I was with Ari, I thought for certain he was dedicated to me. I had no idea the circus that was going on behind my back, with the clown being the ringleader.

When we started our relationship, he swore up and down that he was totally single. Now, grab a pen and paper because you will need this to keep track. After our breakup, mutual acquaintances spilled the tea to me: he had an entire lineup of women in his life.

First, there was Woman A. He was with her when he met me, ditched her to chase me, but kept her simmering on the back burner, confused, wondering where she stood. Enter Woman B, whom he met around the same time as me. He was juggling both Woman A and B while working to secure me as his main love interest. When we became a couple, he even told Woman B she was next in line if we broke up, so she happily and dutifully played her position in the background. Then came Woman C, a friend of his ex-wife and sister, who he started dating while we were still together and kept seeing even after our split, all while courting and expressing his love for me to keep me in the picture while she is thinking he is committed to her. And let's not forget Woman D in Mississippi, his hookup whenever he visited his mom and attended his college activities.

Woman A and C lavished him with money, sports cars, cruises, and trips to Aruba and Dubai, hoping to lock down a permanent spot. Woman B, a known local alcoholic in the area, was happily on standby for his booty calls. He wasn't physically attracted to Woman A or B and wasn't sexually into Woman C. Still, he kept them all around for whatever role they played, maintaining a revolving door that spanned from months to years.

Oh, and then there were a few random stragglers, let's call them Women L, M, N, O, and P, that he picked up along the way, which I also found out about. This is normal behavior for the N-words. They recycle women like plastic water bottles, often rotating past lovers to the present and shifting the present back to the past. He played it like a game of musical chairs, keeping them circling, uncertain, and fighting for a spot, all while he controlled the music. When the song stops, someone is left out, discarded without a second thought.

I was oblivious to the fact this was going on because he was good at concealing his dirt and gaslighting me into believing it isn't what it looks like. In hindsight, the signs were there. However, in present sight, they were not.

Throughout this circus, he constantly accused me of cheating. He would accuse me of everything he did. Now I realize his accusations were my confirmations. My good friend Malaika once told me during one of our conversations, "When your dog starts barking at you, that means someone else is feeding it." He stayed barking, so now I know why. Other supply has entered the chat. He forced arguments frequently to get fed by those who were up for their turn. I have no clue where he found the energy. I wonder where the dick power came from, but people will find a way to feed their addiction by any means necessary, especially when it's used to fight their internal demons.

Narcissists aren't fazed by cheating. They don't feel guilt, just a little shame. Rather than fess up, they justify their cheating as the perfect cure for their misery, which they conveniently blame on their partner.

The emotional abuse became so routine that it no longer fazed me. I had grown accustomed to it. Whenever he flew off the handle over trivial matters, my response was to simply chuckle and brush it off with an "okay." Like clockwork, he would vanish, only to resurface days to a couple of weeks later with the same old nonsense, and everything would revert to its usual state.

He loved to bait me. And he would do it with a disdainful smirk and a sadistic gleam in his eyes. He would call me an elitist when I took the high road and would not fall for the bait. When he would provoke me to lose my peace, this is when I ended up a victim of reactive abuse.

Reactive abuse occurs in toxic relationships when the victim, after enduring prolonged emotional or mistreatment, finally reacts in a way that seems out of character, such as shouting, crying, hitting or throwing something. The narcissist then uses this reaction to blame them, making it appear as though the victim is the one being abusive.

In these relationships, the toxic person constantly manipulates and belittles their partner, causing them to feel worthless and doubt their reality. This continuous stress and emotional pain eventually push the victim to a breaking point, leading them to lash out.

The narcissist then seizes this moment, acting shocked and hurt, and says, "See, this is exactly what I'm talking about when I say you overreact!" This tactic shifts the blame away from the abuser and makes the victim look like the toxic one. It's a way for the N-word to maintain control and avoid taking responsibility for their actions.

I always bottled up my emotions with him, anger, hurt, frustration because I wanted to avoid any drama. Looking back, I realize that wasn't the healthiest approach. I sometimes wonder if that's how women end up on that show *Snapped*. I've never been one to yell, scream, fight, or fuss, preferring instead to keep my composure intact and release it through some form of exercise.

But one argument stands out vividly. It began over something trivial, such as not waking him up when he asked. He had been exhausted, so I let him sleep a bit longer, knowing that our plans for the day were to do nothing. When I woke him up fifteen minutes later, it triggered a huge argument. He was livid, insisting that even though he had no plans, I should have woken him up exactly when he asked. Despite my intention to be considerate, he saw it as a personal offense.

He started yelling, and for the first time, I yelled back. His voice rose, my voice rose, and in a moment of pure frustration, I grabbed a throw pillow from the couch and flung it across the room. It knocked a glass off the table, which shattered on the floor. This was completely out of character for me. I had never thrown anything in anger before, let alone break something. I felt embarrassed and shameful because I pride myself on keeping a level head in tense situations.

But he didn't explode like I expected. Instead, he pulled out his phone, his demeanor shifting to something chillingly calm, his voice suddenly syrupy and sweet. "Look at you," he said, holding the camera steady on me and the shattered glass. "Breaking things in my home like a madwoman. What if one of my kids or the dog stepped on this glass? You're acting foolish and ridiculous, and I'm going to record it all so you can see how you behave. I did nothing to you and right now you have made me fearful and uncomfortable," painting himself as the victim while framing me as unhinged.

I refused to let him control the narrative. Squaring my shoulders, I made sure he got my best angles on camera and began narrating the entire scene, detailing every moment that led to this explosion. He faltered, his smugness crumbling, and abruptly cut the recording. That moment captured the noxious essence of our relationship with me, always striving for peace, bending over backward to avoid conflict, and him, waiting for cracks to form so he could use them against me. My frustration, born of months of bottled emotions, became his weapon, twisting reality until I was the villain in his story. I had tried so hard to remain calm, to keep the chaos at bay, but here I was, raw and vulnerable, my actions distorted into an indictment of my character.

Reactive abuse is real and easy to succumb to. To avoid it, it's crucial to recognize when you're baited to avoid getting drawn into their games. Look out for provocative statements and unsupported accusations as common baiting tactics. Trust your gut. If a comment feels off and continues to bother you, take a step back to re-examine before responding. The best practice is to avoid defending, engaging, and personalizing.

SECTION
THREE
WHEN IT ALL
FALLS APART

CHAPTER 6:

SEX AS POWER - DEVALUATION AS CONTROL

"You have never truly felt hatred until you've been loved by a narcissist."

There is a lot of emotional labor that is required of you when you're involved with a narcissist, and you will never have psychological stability. Narcissists will love bomb you quickly to lure you in. Once you are hooked, they will chip away at your confidence and self-worth over time by devaluing you. They will devalue their exes to the new partners and the new partner/supply will receive the same mistreatment as their ex-partner. Belittling and degrading is their forte, and they do it in a way that isn't blatant. They are toxic and will have temper tantrums anytime they are questioned, challenged, or faced with feedback and take zero accountability. They will treat you like a child. You will be challenged to express your emotions. You will become hypervigilant about voicing your concerns to avoid the repercussions. It's a grooming tactic where they use little to no effort in silencing you because you silence yourself to prevent the smoke and run from the conflict that would arise. They will always try to test your boundaries to see where they can trespass. The more you allow them to trespass, the more they will push the envelope.

The devaluing process in a narcissistic relationship is a gradual and manipulative tactic used by the narcissist to undermine your self-worth and confidence. Initially, during the idealization phase, the narcissist showers you with love, attention, and affection, making you feel special and valued. However, as the relationship progresses, the narcissist begins to devalue you through various means.

Criticism and gaslighting become common as the narcissist starts to belittle your thoughts, feelings, and actions. The narcissist may deny past events, invalidate your emotions, and portray themselves as the victim. Affection is withheld, leaving you feeling unloved and unworthy.

Manipulation tactics are used to control your behavior and emotions, including guilt-tripping, silent treatment, and threats. The narcissist compares you unfavorably to others, fostering feelings of inferiority and insecurity. Devaluing behavior occurs in a cyclical pattern, alternating with periods of idealization and love bombing, creating confusion and emotional turmoil.

Overall, the devaluing process aims to break down your sense of self-worth and independence, making you more dependent on the narcissist for validation and approval. It is a calculated strategy used by the narcissist to maintain power and control in the relationship.

I believe the role I played for him was being eye candy, a sexual partner, and a well-known, well-liked figure. Ari didn't really like me much because I tried to set boundaries and had expectations for him to follow through. When things didn't seem right, I made attempts to speak up instead of staying silent, which led to our frequent arguments. When I wasn't in the mood for confrontation, I would be silent. I was constantly put in a position where I either had to hold him accountable to meet my needs or stay quiet to avoid his hostile responses. I did both. But being quiet meant accepting his disrespect, which only fed his ego and worsened things.

The devaluing that Ari delivered began with mild criticism and occasional visits to the principal's office but eventually escalated into heated arguments over trivial matters. Every 10-15 days, like clockwork, I experienced devaluation. I never had to look at a calendar because my body and symptoms would tell me the date. It became so predictable that my body and mind could sense it coming. By day 7, I would start getting headaches so severe that I sought medical help and was eventually prescribed a daily headache-preventative medication. These headaches were so disruptive that they dictated my plans and activities, causing me to decline invitations in anticipation of the pain. For instance, if I was invited to an event on day 6, I wouldn't accept it because I knew my body would go through the cycle of the trauma response by the next day.

Additionally, by day 8 or 9, I would also experience heart palpitations because I knew the ball was going to drop in a few more days. My body was trained to anticipate the bi-weekly whirlwind. Week after week, my body would enter a state of fight or flight due to the toxic cycle I was engulfed in.

When your body goes into "fight or flight" mode, it's essentially preparing you to deal with a perceived threat or danger. This occurs when one may experience anxiety. This response is controlled by your nervous system, which triggers a series of physiological changes to help you either confront the threat (fight) or flee from it (flight).

Physiologically, your body releases stress hormones like adrenaline and cortisol, which increase your heart rate, blood pressure, and breathing rate, providing you with a surge of energy. Your muscles tense up, your senses become sharper, and your blood flow increases to essential organs like the brain and muscles while decreasing to non-essential functions like digestion. This heightened state of arousal prepares you to react quickly and decisively to the threat. Over time, these elevated hormone levels can suppress immune function, making the body more susceptible to inflammation and autoimmune conditions. I will dive deeper into this in a later chapter.

The unrelenting stress caused by emotional abuse can create an environment of low-grade inflammation in the body, which is a known trigger for autoimmune diseases such as lupus, rheumatoid arthritis, and Hashimoto's thyroiditis. Victims often suppress their emotions to avoid conflict, leading to unresolved tension that manifests physically as fatigue, chronic pain, or digestive issues. When this mind-body disconnect persists, it can aggravate or even initiate autoimmune conditions.

As a result of him causing my body constantly to go into fight or flight mode, I then developed digestive problems with a myriad of symptoms. Within 2 years, I went from taking zero medications to several, like digestive enzymes, beta blockers for high blood pressure, and headache preventatives, to handle the symptoms I later realized were a result of constant emotional and mental abuse. I had no idea why I was developing issues when I have always been incredibly healthy. To my surprise, those symptoms would disappear when we had our short "breaks" or time away. This man was slowly killing me, and I didn't know it.

Time went on and we were off and on bi-weekly. As the months progressed in this toxic situation of a relationship, I began to realize I was being viewed as an object, being valued by only what I could provide or how I made him feel.

Because the narcissist constantly fights internal battles and is emotionally challenged, there must be some sort of coping mechanism. I strongly believe sex was his. Emotionally challenged individuals require constant validation and that was one of the ways I validated him.

Having sex several times a day became a daily routine. He was a satyromaniac. He was insatiable, driven by an unrelenting hunger that went beyond desire, it was a compulsion, a relentless need to dominate and consume. His charm was a weapon, disarming and intoxicating, but beneath the surface lay a darker truth. Every touch, every glance, was calculated, feeding an insidious addiction. He wasn't capable of connection or intimacy, only conquest. The bedroom became a battleground, where his need for control blurred the lines between passion and possession. His appetite was never satisfied, leaving me drained, hollow, and questioning whether I was ever more than just another notch in his endless pursuit of validation.

He had an abnormal, contemptible sexual appetite that I never knew was physically possible from any human. He was able to have an unlimited number of orgasms daily. After one orgasm, he only required a short amount of downtime to recoup before the next one, and I was up for the challenge. At times, downtime wasn't required. I know what you're thinking, but no, he was not taking any enhancement medications. His libido was so intense that I sometimes wondered if he would also be getting pleasured by men.

One night, while in the act, he asked me to open my mouth. When I did, he spit in it. Unlike it would be in a healthier relationship, it wasn't romantic, it wasn't sexy, and it wasn't freaky, it was degrading. I knew it was his way of trying to exercise control in a situation he felt weak in. Disgusted to ingest his poison, I proceed to kiss him to feed his poison right back to him. When I asked him what made him do that, he smirked, "I just wanted to see what you would do if I did it. How did it make you feel?" I lied and replied, "I liked it." But it really made me feel disrespected and lower than the price of air fryers at a Black Friday sale at Walmart. I refused to give him the satisfaction of knowing that, though.

I became his personal sex machine and his human blow-up doll. I stayed ready, so I didn't have to get ready. A typical 24-hour period consisted of being bent over in the middle of cooking his dinner on the stove, bent over while brushing my teeth while taking a shower, pants being slid down while changing a light bulb or reaching for something, and continuously throughout the night while laying on my side as I was sleeping. Eight to ten encounters would be normal. I would be a walking zombie the following day, finding difficulty in performing professionally at work.

Sex became a task, a duty, like a dirty job with no pay and no benefits that I had to fulfill so I would not get fired. It was a job

I didn't like, but a job that I needed and a job I wasn't ready to replace. As toxic and robotic as it was, something about his insatiable craving for me and his addiction to my body turned me on. Sex was the only time I could defeat him, make him my bitch, and have him show his vulnerability and submit to me. Sex was the only time I was able to dominate him, take out my frustrations, and express myself to him in an aggressive way without any recourse. So, as a result, I developed a toxic addiction to those moments of overpowering him without consequences versus the lackluster sexual acts themselves. Making love, left the building early on. We f—ked.

Aside from my lady part being stroked, it was the only time my ego got stroked too. He would constantly praise my performance, and I knew the only weakness he had for me was my body. It was the only time I felt desired by him, and shamefully, it was okay with me. It was something. Something outside of the random moments of love bombing after a breakup.

Despite feeling overwhelmed like an unpaid little sex worker, I struggled not to refuse him, fearing it would push him to seek satisfaction elsewhere, not knowing he was seeking it anyway. He managed to gaslight and manipulate me by shifting the blame for his insatiable sexual appetite onto me, claiming that my mere presence was irresistible to him and he was addicted to me. He stated that his love for me and attraction to me created his insatiable appetite and that no one was ever able to learn his "places" or please him but me. He insisted that he wasn't ever like this with anyone else, but taking his word for it was hard. It got to a point where I would purposely downplay my appearance around him and do everything in my power not to turn him on, hoping for some rest, which never occurred.

If I was to ever tell him no, he would tell me that I shouldn't deny him. He would tell me that nothing hurts him more than if he is denied his needs and desires by the woman he loves and wants to spend the rest of his life with. He told me denying him, despite already complying several times, was selfish when all he wanted to do is show me love and affection. It didn't matter if I was tired or not feeling well. I was expected not to deny him of his unquenchable thirst.

If I did say no, I would then receive an attitude, a sit-down hour-long discussion over his needs and my selfishness, or the silent treatment. I wasn't recognized as an individual with my own needs or emotions. My feelings and desires were unimportant to him. I was continuously objectified. In the beginning, he may have appeared caring to gain my trust, but once that was established, his true selfishness emerged.

I have always had a heavy menstrual cycle, but out of nowhere, I started having the heaviest periods of my life, lasting 8-9 days and to a point where I would bleed through my clothes. Instead of receiving love, care, and support, he would complain because of the inability to feed his sexual appetite during those days. I would fear I would have to tolerate being cheated on due to not being able to fulfill his relentless sexual demands. Of course, I couldn't continue like this, so I sought medical attention. Due to my age, the doctor would no longer allow me to take birth control pills and recommended I get a hysterectomy. Terrified of such an invasive procedure, I researched and found a procedure to assist with the fibroids and bleeding. This procedure would decrease or completely get rid of my menstrual cycle. I immediately scheduled the surgery in early February and was told to wait until the end of the month to resume sexual activities. We all know what day is in February, Valentine's Day.

Valentine's Day would always be just another day on the calendar for me. Previous relationships had regularly spoiled me with constant gestures of affection, flowers, dinners, thoughtful acts, and gifts, making Valentine's Day feel redundant. The clichéd offerings of overpriced menus, crowded restaurants, Russell Stover chocolates, and stuffed animals held no appeal to me. But in this relationship, Valentine's Day took on a new significance. With little acknowledgment throughout the year, I found myself eagerly anticipating the chance for some recognition and affection.

After coaxing and convincing him to make plans for Valentine's Day, he finally booked an Airbnb for a cozy staycation in the city, showering me with three dozen flowers and planning a lovely dinner with a greeting card with sweet words. I was shocked because this was out of character for him. However, despite my reminder about my doctor's orders to avoid sex for another 15 days due to recovery, the weekend turned into an unexpected marathon of intimacy, with several quickies and sexual encounters each day. We barely ate or slept. Exhausted and still recuperating, I went along with it, pretending to enjoy it so as not to ruin the weekend I had been looking forward to. By the end, every part of my body, from my neck to my toes, was fatigued. The thought of getting dressed for dinner filled me with dread because all I wanted to do was lay down and sleep and be left alone.

After countless episodes that day, eight to be exact, we were running late for our dinner reservation. I was excited to see where he was taking me. As we were leaving the Airbnb late for dinner, I reached for the doorknob, only to have him stop me with a tender gaze and a smile. He stared deep into my eyes. He gently caressed my cheek, tilted his head, and leaned in for a passionate kiss, momentarily making me feel cherished and adored. But then, in a sudden shift, he began to unbuckle his belt and slacks, silently signaling for me to drop to my knees by applying pressure and pushing downward on my left shoulder, shattering the illusion of love and affection.

I reminded him we were already running late for our reservation due to us having to re-shower. He proceeded to throw a tantrum and gaslight me by telling me how I do not make him feel special and how he needs to re-evaluate things with us because I am being selfish. Also, how I don't consider his needs and how my selfish acts hurt him after he spent all this money and time planning the weekend. He went on to state how he planned this amazing weekend for me, which is out of the norm for him, and how dare I refuse him more affection. He pulled his pants up with an attitude and sternly said, "Fine, let's go. This is why men cheat." It goes without saying that the ride to dinner was long and silent. I was consumed with mixed emotions. I felt guilty for refusing him on a holiday and ruining a moment. I felt nervous about how terrible a time we would have because of it. I felt angry because who the hell did he think he was talking to. I felt regret for not complying to keep the peace so we could enjoy our dinner. Yet I felt relieved because my body needed to take a break.

During dinner, he made no eye contact, and we had little to no conversation. I forced a dialogue, and of course, he found something to complain about. This time, he was complaining about me joking in the elevator on the way up to the restaurant from the parking garage. Dinner was not enjoyable at all. I was on eggshells, watching what I said to not set him off. After dinner, at bedtime, I mustered up the energy to try to make it up to him, knowing his inability to resist, and he turned his back on me and told me he wasn't interested or in the mood. I was hurt and happy at the same time, but by the morning, continuing endlessly through the afternoon, we spun the block back to pound town for several more rounds until it was dark outside replenishing our energy with bottled water and Doritos.

After coming up for air that evening, I had a nice dinner planned for him. I selected a restaurant we had always discussed trying. I was filled with excitement and anticipating his response knowing he wanted to try this place for a while. We finally arrived.

"This is all I get? The restaurant I took you to was much nicer," he said. He chuckled to make it look like he was joking, but I knew he was serious.

"How about we leave, and I can swing past a drive-through?" I responded because, at this point, I was over it. My mouth has always been slicker than a can of oil when provoked.

"There you go, overreacting again. Can we just enjoy ourselves for once?"

"Again?" I thought to myself, knowing I never overreact.

We stayed and he made sure he ordered 3 top shelf drinks and everything on the menu so my bill could exceed what he spent the previous night.

My Valentine's weekend ended with us checking out and with a lecture on how I am selfish, how I need to let him lead, how he has no control or "influence" over me, and how I won't let him mold me into the wife he desires. Emotionally, physically, and mentally, I was spent. I had no rebuttal to give. He dropped me home, asked for another round in the sheets, gave me a kiss, and left. After he left, I stayed in bed the rest of the night, dreading the entire weekend, weak from my pornographic performance and mental beat down when I should have been relaxing, being pampered and healing from my medical procedure.

The next morning, my phone buzzed with a five-paragraph breakup text. It was full of his usual rhetoric about how I'd hurt him, how I was too independent, and how he couldn't be with someone who denied him his "needs" or refused to let him shape them into his ideal partner. He painted me as selfish while conveniently ignoring the part where I'd catered to his every whim and neglected myself in the process. He discarded me summarizing that he felt he had no influence over me. I was pissed that I made the mistake of catering to this fool only to get dumped after Valentine's Day while being forced into my "sex job" even after requesting imaginary PTO to the boss.

I read the message twice, but instead of sadness, I felt an overwhelming sense of relief. With a calm clarity I hadn't felt in months, I typed back, *"I wish you the best. Take care."*

That was it. No dramatic farewell, no tears, no regrets. Just a quiet acceptance that I'd been set free. For the first time in a long time, I felt light. I went on with my day, finally reclaiming my peace.

Needless to say, he didn't receive the reaction and supply he expected, filled with tears, me questioning why, or the emotions he required for his fix.

The following day, I received a text message that read, "How are you doing?" I responded with, "Great," and ran down the list of things I accomplished. He called that evening, and I didn't answer. The next day, I received a call as if nothing had happened, asking what time we were meeting to attend a movie premiere we had planned on attending together a couple of weeks prior to the fall out. All I could do was shake my head at the audacity. I told him that I was still attending and not with him. He then tried to accuse me of taking another man. Although he didn't deserve to know, I informed him my daughter was attending with me, and he finally backed down after asking me to send him photos afterward because he knew we would be looking nice. He didn't care how we looked. He wanted to make sure I wasn't with another man.

Despite his repeated attempts to draw me back, I stood ten toes down on business, and I stood firm and declined each offer, including his mediocre cooked meals and invitations for dates. However, when he informed me that his mother had been rushed to the hospital, my love for her and my concern for her well-being prompted me to respond. As he continued to keep me updated on her condition, the lines of communication between us reopened. Eventually, I fell weak and joined the clown back at the circus, walking the tightrope again.

The devaluation and manipulation continued off and on. We would be good. He would start an argument, devalue me, discard me and hoover me back only to do it again shortly after. This time, we were not on speaking terms and haven't been for several days. There was a couple we used to double date with frequently as the four of us were friends. It was my friend September's birthday. She was one that he had fooled into thinking he was an upstanding man. She continued to root for us. In a misguided attempt to play cupid, she told me it would mean the world to her if he and I joined her and her man for dinner for her birthday for "old time's sake." They were constantly trying to keep the square intact, but their relationship was as toxic as ours. I declined but she insisted it was important to her, so I agreed to it.

We were all in the same Uber Black and I was looking forward to my wagyu rib eye with garlic butter, Caesar salad, and lobster mac and cheese. The Uber ride was nothing short of excruciating. When we arrived at the restaurant, the atmosphere at dinner was suffocatingly thick, like trying to cut through it with a chainsaw. Every second felt like an eternity, and I found myself dreading the whole ordeal. Seated in a U-shaped booth, I strategically placed my jacket between him and I as a futile attempt to create a physical barrier so our thighs would not touch. As if the discomfort couldn't escalate further, the waiter suggested a group photo, urging us to huddle closer. Of course, I didn't budge.

"Oh, so you can't move in closer to me," he said.

"I'm fine here," I replied.

At that moment, I saw an alert on his phone from a woman labeled GiGi that said, "How is dinner?" with a heart emoji.

I responded with, "So, are you going to let her know how dinner is?"

This is where things went south. Out of the blue, he instantly went from casual to psychotic. He started yelling from the top of his lungs and said, "Damn right, I will let her know. You need to not worry about it."

"I'm not worried about it. I just wanted you to know I saw it, but my apologies. It isn't even my business anymore. My steak and lobster mac are delicious. Just forget I said anything." I replied.

Out of nowhere, I heard, "Fuck you, Bitch, I ought to spit on you Mother Fucker!" He yelled as he pounded his fist on the table, knocking the small items over.

When I looked at him, the eyes staring back at me weren't even his. His brown pupils turned black. It was as though he was looking at me but didn't see me. I had never seen the vein in the middle of his forehead before.

His friend Bill stopped him and told him to chill, and the two of them started to verbally tussle and got in each other's face. I sat there and replied "Wow" and tried to quickly finish the rest of my steak because it was so good, but I was ready to go at that point.

Everyone in the restaurant was staring, while he and his friend were in each other's face going at it. It looked like a scene from a reality show. My friend let me get the last bite of the food and ushered me to the lady's room.

"What on earth was that? What the hell is wrong with his crazy ass?" September asked.

"That is just him being him, but this was the nastiest thing he ever said to me. What I'm not going to do is have relationship issues with a clown I'm not in a relationship with. I'm ready to leave." I tearfully replied.

I apologized to her for him making her birthday dinner a shit show. She apologized to me for suggesting both of us attend together.

He was waiting outside the bathroom door when we came out of the restroom and was apologizing profusely, asking me to forgive him and stating that he had too much to drink. He kept saying, "You know this isn't me. Brown alcohol has this effect on me. You wouldn't understand because you don't drink."

"Yeah, ok," I responded. "That was totally uncalled for. You really showed your ass this time." I said and commenced to go outside to wait for the Uber.

"Can we please talk? I missed you." He said.

"Nah, I'm good," I replied.

The sight and thought of him made me sick to my stomach. I told myself I was done for good. There is no coming back from a man telling me he ought to spit on me. I didn't take his calls, and I didn't respond to his texts. He was very persistent. He sent me flowers, offered me food, and asked if he could take me away for a weekend getaway, and I just wasn't interested. He would call and ask me if we could "cuddle" how he needs me, tell me that the dogs miss me, and please do not leave him. He never took accountability but deflected to alcohol. He refused to back down until we had a conversation. Knowing he wouldn't give up and needing closure, I agreed. His tear-filled apology seemed genuine, but then I realized I was dealing with a master manipulator, and this is what he does. He could easily cry when convenient. He is very conniving, calculating, and convincing. I told him I needed time and space and that is exactly what he wouldn't give me. I also found out that a narcissist will never provide closure. But I was done anyway.

He continued apologizing, tried to court me and I wanted nothing to do with him. I emotionally moved on and was in a good and healthy space. It wasn't until his friend Bill reached out to me to inform me that Ari's father had passed away. Although he mentioned not having a good relationship with his father, I was willing to put everything from that night aside to check on him. I rushed to his aid, held him, consoled him, cooked, helped him clean his home and tried to crack jokes to cheer him up. He asked me to be by his side during the funeral, which was out of town. Although I didn't want to, for several reasons, I couldn't find it in my heart to abandon him.

I flew to his hometown in Mississippi while he drove and the plan was to ride back with him. Not to my surprise, he went from appreciative to a monster in the blink of an eye. I gave him grace and wrote it off as him being consumed with grief, but I knew the minute I returned home I wanted nothing to do with him AGAIN. While he was grieving his father, I was grieving us because I knew without a shadow of a doubt we were finished, and I was not going back. We stayed at his lovely mother's home. We were there for several days. She apologized to me on his behalf for his behavior.

The incident that finalized my feelings was when we were running late doing you know what.

"Can you iron my clothes while I'm in the shower to save time? I suck at ironing. Of all the things you do better than me, ironing is definitely one of them," I said.

"Sure, and hurry up because I need to shower also," he stated.

I rushed out of the shower. I thanked him for ironing my clothes, but he didn't respond.

"Is everything okay?" I asked.

"Let it go," He responded.

I let it go. He didn't.

As we got dressed, his huffing and puffing was like a storm waiting to strike. His every movement was exaggerated, buttoning his shirt with jerky motions, yanking his tie into place with unnecessary force. I watched, puzzled, until he suddenly snapped, his voice sharp and accusing.

"You insulted me," he said, his words cutting through the air like a blade.

WHEN IT ALL FALLS APART

"Wait, what? How?" I asked, genuinely confused.

"You said I iron better than you," he hissed.

I blinked, stunned. "That's... a compliment."

"To you, maybe," he fired back, his voice rising. "But to me, it's an insult. You don't get to decide what's insulting to me."

He was relentless, his tone a mix of anger and wounded pride. He demanded an apology, not caring that I didn't understand why it was necessary. "You don't have to understand! I told you it hurt me. That should be enough, so you need to address my feelings!"

The ride to the wake was a nightmare. He shouted the entire way, his frustration echoing in the confined space of the car. My attempts to reason with him were met with louder accusations. The tighter I clung to my need for clarity, the more unhinged he became. He continued to verbally crash out.

When we arrived at the church, he refused to sit beside me, instead choosing a seat directly in front of mine. The message was clear: He wanted to punish me for issuing a compliment that he felt was insulting. I sat quietly, my gaze fixed on the back of his head as I tried to console him with small gestures, a gentle touch on his shoulder, a whispered word of comfort. He shrugged me off with cold precision, giving me first his silence and then figuratively, his ass to kiss. His anger at me seemed to burn hotter than his grief for his father.

At one point, his sister asked me to sign the guest book. I wrote my name, but when I got to the section labeled *relationship to the deceased,* my pen hovered. None of the options seemed right. *Girlfriend to son? Family friend? Future ex-daughter-in-law?* None of them fit the mess we'd become. So, I left it blank, thinking it was the safest choice.

It wasn't.

When we got back to the car, his fury erupted like a volcano. "You left it blank on purpose!" he screamed, pounding his fist against the dashboard with such force that I flinched.

"What? No, I didn't. It's not even like that!" I firmly stated, but my words only fueled the fire.

"You wanted to embarrass me! You did it to make my family question us! You're trying to disrespect me and kick me when I'm already down!" he roared, his face contorted with rage.

His accusations came in like rapid fire, each one more ludicrous than the last. Spit flew as he screamed, his voice hoarse from yelling. He was relentless, hammering away at me with words meant to break me down.

I tried to explain in my therapeutic voice, keeping my voice steady despite the fear tightening my chest. "I didn't know what to put. I thought leaving it blank would avoid confusion. That's all."

But my calmness only enraged him further. His fists slammed into the dashboard again, and his threats to send me home continued loudly. I felt trapped with no way out.

Silently, I reached for my phone and hit record, knowing he'd later deny this meltdown or twist it into something I'd done wrong.

"Apologize! Right now!" he demanded, his voice cracking with the weight of his fury.

"I... I just need you to understand—" I began, but he cut me off abruptly.

"There's nothing to understand! Just say you're sorry!"

I bit my tongue, swallowing the urge to snap back. Anything I said would only become ammunition. I cursed him out several times in my head. I sat in silence, gripping my phone like a lifeline, waiting for the storm to pass. But deep down, I knew the truth. There was no reasoning with him, no way to win. He'd already decided I was guilty, and nothing I said would change his mind. As he continued to yell, I stared out the window, my reflection staring back at me. In that moment, I saw someone tired, drained, and utterly spent. Someone who didn't deserve this.

And I promised myself. *This ends here.*

"This mother fucker is crazy but I'm going to show him grace in case this is his way of grieving." I thought to myself.

We arrived back at his mother's home. His family was aware of his behavior and tried to console me. His acting out was not foreign to them. His sister Tyra tried to console me and apologized to me for his actions. She thanked me for being there. Although his twin, she was nothing like him.

There were no flights that night, so I planned to leave the next day, the actual funeral day. The original plan was to ride back in the car with him and his family. Of course, even after his horrific performance of disrespecting me, he couldn't resist, during bedtime, rolling over in the middle of the night and sex me while I was asleep. Knowing it would only last a whopping 236 seconds, I pretended I was in the REM stage of sleep to avoid prolonging it.

When we woke up, he offered no apologies, yet he tried to pretend like nothing happened and he asked me to stay. I agreed. And to no surprise, after the funeral and burial, he found something else to fight about. He had promised to take me to Greece for my birthday but never lifted a finger to make the plans. He asked me to contribute financially to my birthday gift and I refused. He then blamed me for the high rates and orchestrated his out by conjuring up a frivolous argument and yelled, "I would never take you to Greece because we argue too much!"

It was time to get on the road. Thank goodness it was the last night there, but it was hands down the longest car ride in history, with us not saying one word to each other for several hours.

A couple of weeks passed, and we didn't communicate at all. I was good with that until he reached out to me. I enjoyed the moments of peace but still wondered how he was doing. We chatted, and I thought that was the end, but it wasn't. He commenced to tell me how I abandoned him while he was grieving. I was sensitive to the fact that he lost a parent, so I took that on the chin and didn't want to go back and forth with him.

"I apologize if I made you feel that way," I swore to God that was the last apology he would ever receive from me. He continued to stay in touch with me, even though I truly couldn't stand the way he blinked, the way he spoke, the way his eyebrows didn't connect, the way he breathed, that one gray hair in his jet-black goatee, or the way he chewed his food. Everything about him irritated me and turned me off.

He was on his best behavior in the days and weeks ahead. He was doing all the things I needed him to do early in the relationship. His caring actions and adoring ways were consistent for several weeks. He started doing things around my house, fixing things, and taking me out. He convinced me that losing me was a detriment to him and that he had changed. I began to question if I was wrong about him being a narcissist and held out hope that this new version of him, he was showing me was not temporary.

The bi-weekly discards went away for a few months, and we carried on like we had no issues. I noticed how he would catch himself before he said the wrong thing, before he made me feel a certain type of way. There was never any mention that we were "back together," and I know when we would have our "breaks," he was probably doing his thing, but we were carrying on as if we were back together, but it was different this time. He would go out of his way to keep my attention. He even tried to wow me with his new black Lexus sports car, which I later found out a year later was purchased by the new supply he was seeing while still seeing me. He seemed annoyed that I wasn't impressed by it.

I was not bothered if I didn't hear from him frequently. I enjoyed the peace. I rarely reached out to him first. It was him reaching out to me. The tables turned. I knew I wanted nothing to do with him, and I think he knew, too, but I was still in heal mode, trying to sort out what we were doing, why, and what was going on. I still cared for him but wasn't in love with him nor liked him.

I hung around to see if things would change, despite knowing deep down that I should rip the band-aid off and cut ties.

CHAPTER 7:

CREATING CHAOS — THE TRIANGULATION TRIFECTA

"They turn love into competition and connection into conflict."

Triangulation, the art of manipulating a relationship dynamic by leveraging a third party's opinion or presence, is a favorite trick in the toxic person's playbook. The goal is to instill jealousy and insecurity or create a competitive environment to control, unarm, and dominate their partner. This sneaky tactic can also conjure up messy love triangles, leaving you feeling like you're on shaky ground.

The process of triangulation usually unfolds in several stages. They are masters of this game. They'll happily drag you into conversations with strangers, coworkers, exes, friends, or family to stir up feelings of envy and doubt in you. This could be through comparisons or seeking validation.

Next, they use the attention or presence of that person to create feelings of jealousy or inadequacy in you. This could involve flirtation, hints, or explicit comparisons designed to undermine your confidence. It can also include misleading their current supply that the previous supply is still interested simply to keep the new supply on her toes.

As the triangulation persists, the narcissist erodes your confidence in the relationship by insinuating that you are inadequate. This undermines your self-esteem and fosters a reliance on the narcissist for validation and acceptance.

When faced with the dilemma of choosing between two women, a narcissist typically opts not to choose either one. Instead, he selects both. If a narcissist has the opportunity to maintain relationships with two primary sources simultaneously, he will seize it. They will just play two different roles in his life.

The woman with the strongest boundaries, who refuses to tolerate toxic behavior, emerges as the victor. She is the one who dictates the terms and has more control over the narcissist. This was the position I placed myself in when I was emotionally done with him.

The narcissist doesn't actively choose, rather, he embraces both options if given the chance. This is how triangulation occurs. I'm sure I played that role after walking away from him yet still allowing him to keep in touch with me. It's more common to include an old supply and a new supply. While the new supply is being groomed and molded for toxicity, the old supply is figuring out how to let go. Trust me, if you were with a narcissist, you were in a one-sided open relationship the day he told you he wanted to be exclusive.

Does the narcissist find happiness with the new supply they cheated on you with or married? Far from it. The new supply was secondary, the dirty, hidden secret. They were never the first choice, they were the clandestine option. Whether or not they marry them or stay with them for a while doesn't matter. The new supply becomes a pawn in the narcissist's game, blamed for their loss of you. It's a never-ending spherical cycle.

The narcissist will do everything to try to get the new supply to mimic you by changing their appearance, the way they dress, and even their mannerisms. They will throw you in the new supply's face to make her feel insecure and inferior with the purpose of creating doubt to keep her vigilant and pressed.

Looking back, it's so clear how he thrived on keeping me off balance, always questioning my place in his life. Aside from manipulation, his favorite tool was triangulation, and his ex-wife was his weapon of choice. He would casually drop comments like, "She still wants me, you know," or "If I gave her the chance, she'd be back in a heartbeat." These statements were designed to unsettle me, to plant seeds of insecurity. At the same time, he made a point of parading me in front of her whenever the opportunity arose. He even mentioned one time, "She's going to be sick when she sees how beautiful you are," while chuckling. He seemed to relish the chance to create tension, but it never had the desired effect, not on her, at least.

His ex-wife carried herself with an upbeat, confident elegance that only amplified my discomfort. She was friendly and composed, completely unfazed by his attempts to stir the pot. It was as if she saw right through him and decided he wasn't worth the energy. I'll never forget one moment after his father's funeral, standing in a crowded room. I caught her eye from across the space, and she gave me a look that said everything without a word: *Better you than me.* It wasn't mocking or mean, it was almost a warning wrapped in resignation. In that moment, I understood the truth. She wasn't pining for him like he said she was. She wasn't plotting a way back into his life. He was just using her name and their past to keep me uneasy, and it worked.

I'd bet anything he did the same thing with the woman who came after me. I could already imagine the lies he fed my successor, flipping the script this time, saying I was still hung up on him, desperate to win him back. It was his game, his cycle, and I was just one of many pawns he played with. But now, the thought of it makes me laugh bitterly. Silly rabbit, indeed. His tricks only worked because I cared, because I hadn't yet seen him for what he truly was. And in the end, that's all they were:

cheap tricks designed to keep the spotlight on him, no matter how many lives he disrupted in the process.

The covert narcissist has a pattern of devaluing their exes to their new partners, and eventually, the new partner experiences the same mistreatment as the narcissist's previous partner. In the end, you'll likely find yourself subjected to the same abuse. It's a cycle where you could eventually become the ex they disparage to their next source of attention. That's why it's crucial to remain vigilant about their love-bombing tactics whenever their actions don't match their words.

It's important to understand that whoever the narcissist is involved in their triangulation tactics is also being manipulated by your relationship with the narcissist. Essentially, everyone involved is being used as pawns in the narcissist's game. One reason narcissists tend to incessantly discuss their past relationships, especially in the early stages of a new relationship, is because they perceive each partner as interchangeable. To them, you are not seen as unique but merely as the latest role in their ongoing dysfunctional narrative.

Let's talk about after you're done and there's a new supply. The new supply will know all about you. They will stalk your social media. He may post her to annoy you and boost her ego and to make her feel like she has one up on you when the real tea is that she is checking your social media because he used you to make her insecure. So now she is checking to see if he likes your posts or if there are any signs that you're in contact. She is taking notes on how to become you because she knows he hasn't mentally left you. At this stage, she thinks she has won the prize and has a leg up on you, while at the same time, he is working overtime to keep you as a presence in his life.

The honorable mention, aka new supply believes their love surpasses yours, unknowingly engaging in a silent competition with you when the only thing she is competing for is going to be her own sanity and self-worth. They think things are going to be different from what you had with them, but they're just going to get the same treatment. They think they can fix whatever happens and show this person the love she thinks he deserves.

Remember, he turned her against you, so her goal is to beat you. She will soon find out.

Speaking of new supply, the supply isn't new. More than likely, she was lurking in the background of your relationship, waiting for her turn during your discard. One thing you cannot do is concern yourself with what he is doing or who he is with. You can't be concerned with how things are going with him and the backup because it doesn't matter. He is running the same weak game and serving up the exact same toxic cocktail on ice to his new prey. You just have to celebrate that it is no longer you and understand that it isn't a reflection of your worth. You are much better off, and sadly, someone else is the victim now.

CHAPTER 8:

MR. CONTROL FREAK AND MISS HYPERVIGILANT

"No one gets more upset than a narcissist being accused of something they did."

We were called middle-aged Barbie and Ken. There was no denying that, side by side, we looked great together. We had a contagious chemistry that others admired when we were in their presence. Things were only great with us when I learned how to react and respond to life on his terms. I was getting to the point where his gaslighting and manipulation were becoming easy to spot. I was also getting to the point of becoming a subject matter expert on narcissism to figure out a way NOT to get away from him, but how to co-exist with him. Also, with that same knowledge, I knew how to beat him, how to annoy him, and how to get under his skin. It took very little effort.

For a moment, I liked it there. Watching him swallow his own bitter pill was almost as sweet as dessert. I found myself becoming as toxic as he was. He deserved to get a taste of his own medicine, and I didn't mind serving it up cold. I started to intentionally gaslight him, disagree with him, and subtly devalue him. I knew it was becoming a problem when I started to look forward to screwing with him as payback, and the back and forth became my changed reality. It felt like a dark, forbidden game, and it felt so good to finally win. At least, that's what I told myself. I was so engulfed in the venom he spewed that I was not only brewing it, but I was sipping my own toxic tea. It was as though I was drowning in the toxic pool of quicksand, unable to reach the surface. I had given up and didn't care about being the bigger person. Misery loved company and lord knows I was miserable. I thought I couldn't sink any lower, so why not embrace the darkness? Each effort to break free only seemed to sink me further into chaos. I needed way more than a life jacket. I needed strength, resilience, and self-preservation.

I couldn't bear the thought of becoming the same beast I was fighting with, loving, and trying to change. The bitterness in my voice, the sharpness in my words, the growing urge to strike back were all warning signs that his poison was spreading. I despised what I was becoming. It was as if his chaos had taken root in me, feeding on my emotions and thriving in my exhaustion. But even in the midst of the madness, something deep inside me screamed for a reset. A part of me refused to let him win, to let him turn me into him.

Thank God for self-awareness. It was my anchor, the small but powerful spark that reminded me who I was before him, and who I refused to stop being. That clarity, faint as it felt at times, was my lifeline. I had to get a grip before I spiraled completely, before I lost myself. I wouldn't let him steal my light. Not this time.

The narcissist will dictate how you feel, what you think, what you want, and who you are. They'll inform you about your emotions, whether you're sad, happy, or scared. They'll assert what your preferences are, what you like and dislike, even when you're unsure. They'll define your pain, whether physical or emotional, and interpret your experiences for you. They'll determine your relationships, who you trust and who you don't. They'll control your perceptions of love, abuse, and your own reality. In doing so, the narcissist takes command of your thoughts, emotions, and actions. Again, it is done so subtly that you won't realize it while it's happening until you're already in deep.

Remember, this manipulation isn't your fault. They're skilled at this game. You trusted them, and they exploited that trust to maintain control. But your thoughts, feelings, and choices belong to you. Trust yourself and remember you're not alone facing this manipulation.

I would look at my N-word and have a merry-go-round of thoughts cross my mind as I looked at him and smiled but thinking the opposite of what my face said.

"Geesh, he is so miserable. Is he ever satisfied and happy?"

"This is no doubt the most cynical human on the planet."

"Look at those fake tears."

"I must get out of this. Why am I here?"

"Is he really going off on me for no reason?"

"What the hell is wrong with him?"

"Which character am I going to get today?"

"He isn't even attractive to me anymore."

"Is he really having a tantrum over my social media post?"

"He disgusts me right now."

It wasn't until months of research and reflection that I realized his only goal was to create turmoil and engage in conflict with me to distract himself from his inner issues. The best decision was not to play the game. I later learned that the best choice wasn't to concede in the argument but to never take the bait in the first place.

Not to age myself, but I used to play this game called hot potato as a kid. Participants sit in a circle and pass an object (typically a potato or ball) around while music plays. The catch is that whoever is holding the object when the music stops is "out" and must leave the circle. The game continues until only one player remains. The excitement of hot potato lies in the suspense and frantic passing of the object as players try to avoid being caught with it when the music stops. It's a game of quick reflexes, strategy, and sometimes a bit of luck as players try to pass the "hot potato" to someone else before time runs out.

Blame shifting with a narcissist is like a twisted game of hot potato, where the narcissist skillfully deflects responsibility for their actions onto their partner. It's a manipulative tactic used to evade accountability and maintain their inflated sense of superiority and self-image. They will portray themselves as faultless and virtuous while casting their partner as the villain. They may manipulate situations, distort facts, or outright deny their wrongdoing to shift blame away from themselves.

Challenging a narcissist will never turn out well for you. It can cause narcissistic injury, which in turn can cause a narcissistic rage. They go to great lengths to hide their vulnerability and flaws. When these vulnerabilities are exposed, they are challenged or corrected, or when they're confronted with their own shortcomings, it can shatter their carefully constructed self-image. When they feel criticized, rejected or not given the admiration or validation they believe they deserve, they will unleash their fury upon you.

Narcissistic injury is like poking a balloon full of hot air with a tiny pin. It's that moment when someone bruises a narcissist's ego, and they burst into an over-the-top reaction. When a narcissist gets hurt, it's not just a bruise, it's a full-blown crisis. They might pout and throw a tantrum. It's like watching a diva have a meltdown over a broken nail. The slightest criticism or perceived insult sends them into a tailspin because, underneath all that bravado, their self-esteem is as sturdy as a one-legged chair.

Narcissistic rage is an intense emotional reaction characterized by anger, aggression, or hostility when a narcissist's ego or sense of superiority is threatened, challenged, or undermined. Narcissistic rage can manifest in various ways, from verbal outbursts and yelling to physical aggression or manipulative behavior. It can be unpredictable, leaving you feeling intimidated, confused, or emotionally overwhelmed. Narcissistic rage serves as a defense mechanism for them to protect their fragile self-esteem and maintain their false self-image.

Always remember it's not you, it's them.

They avoid taking responsibility for their actions at all costs and will never admit fault. Even when they know they're wrong, they insist on being right to conceal their shame. When confronted about their behavior, narcissists immediately shift blame onto others, deflecting any accountability. This behavior stems from their inner misery and self-criticism, which they keep hidden. Narcissists prefer to shift blame onto others to feel better about themselves rather than face the consequences of their actions. It's easier for them to blame-shift than to take ownership and apologize. They also do not argue to resolve conflict. They argue to create conflict.

The double bind is also prevalent in toxic relationships. A double bind is an advanced form of manipulation that traps you in a no-win situation. It involves setting up conflicting expectations or demands, leaving you feeling damned if you do and damned if you don't.

What happens is that they will create a scenario where they present you with two options, both of which lead to negative consequences. For example, they may demand constant attention and affection while also accusing you of being needy or clingy. Alternatively, they might expect space but then label you as distant or uncaring if they try to respect those boundaries. They will create emotional unrest with conflicting expectations.

No matter which option you choose, you're met with criticism, blame, or manipulation from their toxic ass. This constant state of uncertainty and anxiety will wear down your self-esteem and confidence, leaving you feeling confused and emotionally drained. It's like being caught between a rock and a hard place, with no way to escape unscathed.

They do this to maintain control and power over you. By setting up impossible expectations, they ensure that you are always in a state of dependency, seeking validation and approval from them. This dynamic reinforces their sense of superiority and dominance in the relationship. In addition to the conflicting expectations, they will double down with gaslighting tactics to further confuse and disorient you and deny and minimize their actions in creating a double bind, making you doubt your own perceptions and reality. This is what keeps you trapped in the toxic dynamic, making it difficult to break the abuse cycle.

My N-word would double-bind me often. He would insist on more quality time together, yet when I obliged, he would tell me I was smothering him. When I gave him space, he would accuse me of neglecting him, denying him of his needs or not caring and investing in the relationship. Then, he would intentionally isolate me and show back up like nothing had changed. When I would ask him, "What do you want from me?" he would respond with, "I want you to let me lead you." Lead was obviously synonymous with control. Regardless of what I did, I was met with disapproval and blame.

Recognizing this control tactic is crucial for you to break free and reclaim your self-esteem and independence.

There's no reasoning with him. He will never admit fault, not just with me, but with anyone. Attempting to reason with a narcissist is like trying to play chess with a pigeon. They'll knock over all the pieces, take a crap on the board, then strut around like a peacock as if they've won. Talking only provides them with more ammunition to gaslight, manipulate, and inflict their toxins upon you. You must stop thinking you can talk your way out of a narcissistic abuse relationship because you can't. The only solution is making a plan to escape, however, you need to do it, and by any means necessary. Talking will keep you trapped in this relationship for months, years, or even decades. Unless you truly understand what is going on, you can't out-manipulate a narcissist, and you don't want to. While you speak from a place of authenticity, they twist your words to their advantage, always seeking to break you down, not heal the relationship.

I had to frequently thank him for miniscule contributions or else I would be called ungrateful. I had to continuously remind myself to stroke his ego, or I would be accused of never uplifting him or making him feel good. I found myself doing things simply for his acceptance. I continuously set myself on fire to keep him warm.

Many of our arguments stemmed from politely correcting him when he was wrong. He hated that, so I stopped. When I wouldn't correct him, he would ask, "Did you know that XYZ......" and I would say, "Yes." And he would go off and say, "Why didn't you tell me? You want me to look stupid."

When I corrected him, he would argue me down and be as wrong as a three-dollar bill. When I produced the data or receipts to corroborate what I was saying, showing he was incorrect, he would have a tantrum and stop speaking to me. So, no matter how wrong he was, I would respond with, "Wow, you're so smart. I didn't know that. Thanks for letting me know." No matter how erroneous his arguments were, I would appease him by praising his intelligence and thanking him for enlightening me. I still can't believe I let myself sink so low. The things we do for our peace.

Narcissists fly into a rage when you stand up for yourself, especially after they've been critical and accusatory. They respond with explosive tantrums and attacks, behaving like entitled bullies who expect to say and do as they please without repercussion. In their eyes, you have no right to defend yourself. They demand silence, compliance, and agreement with their every word, refusing to tolerate any response or critique. While they hold others to strict standards, they never accept accountability for their own actions. When they do indeed issue an apology, it is not accountability. It's used as manipulation.

In a toxic relationship, neither vigilance nor hypervigilance is ideal in the long term. While vigilance involves being watchful and attentive to potential signs of danger or manipulation, hypervigilance takes this to an extreme, resulting in a constant state of heightened alertness and anxiety.

Ideally, in a healthy relationship, vigilance may be appropriate to maintain awareness of any red flags or concerning behaviors. However, hypervigilance, characterized by excessive vigilance and anxiety, can be detrimental to one's mental and emotional well-being.

Instead of perpetuating hypervigilance, individuals in toxic relationships must seek support, set boundaries, and prioritize their own well-being. This may involve seeking therapy, establishing a support network, and developing coping strategies to manage stress and anxiety.

Staying hypervigilant in my toxic relationship was both a blessing and a curse. On one hand, it helped me anticipate potential dangers, protect myself from further harm, and maintain a sense of control in an unpredictable and volatile environment. It served as a survival mechanism, allowing me to stay one step ahead of his emotional abuse and minimize the risk of being blindsided by their manipulation.

On the other hand, hypervigilance took its toll on me, both emotionally and physically. Hypervigilance became my constant companion, lurking in the background of every interaction. It was as if I wore invisible glasses, constantly scanning for any subtle shift in mood or tone that could signal upcoming conflict. My head lived on a swivel. Every raised eyebrow, every sigh, every slight change in demeanor sent alarm bells ringing in my mind. I found myself walking on eggshells, always on guard, always ready to appease and accommodate, to avoid setting off his unpredictable temper. I would sometimes challenge him, but I learned the hard way it was an uphill battle. I was always tense, anxious, and second-guessing my words and actions to ensure they wouldn't provoke a negative reaction. It was exhausting, draining me of my energy and sense of self. But despite my best efforts to anticipate and mitigate his outbursts, I often found myself blindsided by his sudden rage or criticism. It was as if no amount of vigilance could protect me from the emotional rollercoaster of the relationship.

However, it also took its toll on my emotional well-being. It led to heightened stress, and exhaustion as I constantly felt on edge and overwhelmed by the demands of hyper-awareness. I also felt at times that staying hypervigilant distorted my perception of reality, making it difficult for me to trust my own judgment or discern between genuine threats and perceived dangers.

In the end, hypervigilance kept me trapped in a cycle of fear and dependency, unable to break free from the toxic grip he had over me. It was only when I learned to trust my own instincts and prioritize my own well-being that I was able to begin the journey toward healing and liberation.

I avoided showing strong emotions or reactions, such as anger, frustration, or sadness, in response to his behavior or attempts to bait me. I kept a calm, unbothered tone while avoiding confrontational language or gestures that could add more fuel to his fire and aggression. Expressing myself was becoming impossible. I became the human embodiment of grace under fire. While he would be mid-tantrum, spewing his venom with spit flying out of his mouth, I would look at him and respond with, "Are you okay?"

I became a pro using the gray rock technique. Gray rocking, a.k.a. "respond, don't react," is like playing dead for drama-loving predators. It's the art of turning yourself into the human equivalent of beige paint, boring, neutral, and impossible to emotionally engage with. When dealing with a narcissist, this technique is a lifeline, helping you keep the peace by giving them zero fuel for their drama fire.

Here's why it works: narcissists live off your reactions. The more you gasp, argue, or look visibly annoyed, the more they thrive. It's their version of a five-star meal. So, gray rocking is all about keeping things bland. When they throw a tantrum or try to bait you, you respond like a rock: cool, unmoved, and distinctly uninteresting.

But let's be clear. Gray rocking isn't the cure for narcissistic abuse. It's more like a survival tactic. True freedom? That's achieved by going no-contact. Think of it like this: if the narcissist's greatest weapon is trapping you in endless, heated conversations, then the ultimate counter is to shut the door on that chat. And if you can't do that, at least keep your reactions minimal, like the world's most unresponsive, unremarkable gray rock. Because in the end, dealing with a narcissist is like playing a game where the only winning move is not to play. When he told me that I wasn't being his peace, I realized that it was because conflict brought him peace. And I was taking that peace from him by avoiding the conflict.

He was making cosmetic upgrades in his home. He kept trying to get me to help him paint his house. He tried to manipulate me by telling me he wanted me to paint because I would always have a lasting memory in his home and every time, he looked at the walls I painted, he would think of me. Early in the relationship, I would have jumped at the chance and put on overalls and go to work. Once I knew the game, my response was, "I'm not available at the moment for that task. Maybe another time." There are probably several females with a painted wall in that house. No, thank you. I'm happy to remove myself from the lineup.

I provided a non-committal response and did not immediately comply with his request. I asserted boundaries for the first time because I was truly starting to not give a damn. The psychological warfare that I was submerged in was becoming exhausting.

"You continue to deny me of my needs. You can be so selfish at times," he would say.

"I understand and respect your perspective on that." I would reply while eating my chips.

"Well, what are you going to do about it?" He would ask.

"I will figure it out."

See what I did there? I acknowledged his feelings without engaging in self-blame or defensiveness to maintain emotional detachment.

My days were lived in constant FOG. Not the fog you experience on a humid day but Fear, Obligation, and Guilt. I have always been somewhat fearless but in this situation, I was completely vulnerable and let my guard down. I was instilled with fear through intimidation and coercion, mainly stemming from the anticipation of punishment, abandonment, or retaliation if I didn't comply with his requests or cater to his needs. Fear tactics can include verbal abuse. There was never any physical violence, but it was a large degree of psychological manipulation designed to instill a sense of dread and powerlessness within me.

He often imposed a sense of obligation on me, making me feel responsible for meeting his every need or fulfilling his demands. He created a dynamic where I felt compelled to prioritize his desires and needs over my own well-being, sacrificing my own needs and boundaries in the process. Guilt-tripping, emotional blackmail, and manipulation tactics were regularly used to reinforce this sense of obligation.

He enjoyed exploiting my feelings of guilt to maintain control over me. He would use guilt-inducing statements, passive-aggressive behavior, or blame-shifting tactics to try to make me feel responsible for his actions or emotions, which caused me to internalize self-blame, even for things that were not my fault. Recognizing and addressing these dynamics was essential for me to break free from the cycle of abuse and reclaim my independence and well-being.

Ultimately, the goal is to move towards a healthier relationship dynamic or to safely exit the toxic relationship altogether, where vigilance is balanced with self-care, self-love, and self-empowerment.

Navigating conflict and control in a relationship with a narcissist can be incredibly challenging and emotionally draining. These individuals thrive on conflict and manipulation, so it's important to avoid getting drawn into their games. Getting drawn in their games will send you down the rabbit hole. Take it from me. Refrain from (JADE), Justifying, Arguing, Defending, or Explaining yourself in response to their accusations or criticisms.

Instead, assertively state your boundaries and disengage from the conversation if necessary. A narcissist's accusations are also confessions. Preserve your sanity!

CHAPTER 9:

GONE, BUT NOT REALLY – DISCARDING AND HOOVERING

"The best gift a narcissist can ever give you is the gift of goodbye"

Narcissistic abuse unfolds in multiple phases. There is Idealization, Devaluation, Discard, and Hoover. The phases then repeat themselves. The painful discard phase in a toxic relationship is like having the rug pulled out from under you, leaving you feeling like crap. It's the moment when the narcissistic partner, who once showered you with affection and validation, suddenly turns cold, distant, and indifferent and it could be for no reason at all. At times, while you are devastated, they have no intention of permanently leaving, they just want to see you squirm.

A narcissist will never forgive you for exposing their truth on what THEY did to YOU. Once you see behind the mask and recognize them for who they really are, you're no longer valuable to them. In their eyes, you're ruined, damaged by your awareness of their lies. If you refuse to take the blame for their appalling behavior or resist their relentless gaslighting, they'll see no point in staying. It's far easier for them to discard you and latch onto someone new, someone who still sees the illusion. They'll leave without hesitation, because narcissists don't love, bond, or connect in any meaningful way. Their sole focus is on protecting their image and surrounding themselves with people who will mirror back their delusion of greatness.

The moment you start to disagree with them, the second you begin to stand up for yourself, the covert narcissist's true nature emerges. They don't see it as a disagreement, they see it as a personal attack, a betrayal of the power they've carefully cultivated over you. Your independence is a threat to their control, and in an instant, they'll discard you, pretending the bond was never there. The sweet words they once whispered turn into cold silence, and suddenly, you're no longer worth their time because in their world, it's all about dominance, and your defiance is their failure.

They are willing to sever ties and abandon relationships with anyone rather than admit to any wrongdoing or abusive behavior and offer an apology. This includes close family members and even their own children. For a narcissist, nothing is more crucial than maintaining complete control over the narrative, their revised version of events. This narrative is everything to them, and they will never accept responsibility for their actions. If you refuse to conform to their distorted reality, you will be discarded. Whether you're their parent, sibling, spouse, or even their own child, they will discard you if you insist on accountability and an apology. This is a non-negotiable stance for them, regardless of who you are. Don't get me wrong, there may be fleeting moments where an apology is offered, but it is not sincere. If an apology is offered, there is definitely a motive behind it, and you will be constantly reminded of it.

Emotionally, the impact of this discard could be devastating. You're left dealing with a whirlwind of emotions – confusion, betrayal, grief, and loss. You may find yourself questioning your worth, your sanity, and the validity of the entire relationship. The abrupt withdrawal of love and attention leaves a void in your heart, leaving you feeling hollow and alone.

They may vilify you, devalue your worth, or even discard you callously without any closure or explanation. This leaves you feeling rejected, invalidated, and disposable as if your entire existence was nothing more than a temporary convenience to them.

The emotional impact of the discard phase can be long-lasting and profound, affecting your self-esteem, your ability to trust others, and your overall sense of identity. It's a traumatic experience that can leave scars that take time and effort to heal. Yet, to them, it's no more serious than putting the garbage can out on trash day. But despite the pain, surviving the discard phase is a testament to your strength, resilience, and capacity for growth. It's an opportunity to reclaim your power, rebuild your life, and rediscover your worth beyond the toxic confines of the relationship.

I found myself discarded bi-monthly. On a good month, it would be only once. Each time I chose not to fight it, I didn't question it. I went quietly without knocking anything over on my way out or making a dramatic scene. I became immune to the cycle, finding a strange mix of stress and humor in the predictability of it all. All because I knew he couldn't and wouldn't let me go standing. I knew he thrived on my anguish. He wanted me to go grabbling and in tears, and I would never give him the pleasure. He wanted me to question why and ask what I could do to make it better, and I refused because deep down, I knew he was as bonded and entangled to the trauma and toxicity as I was.

Without fail, I found myself discarded after each argument, seemingly orchestrated by him, so I avoided confrontation and conflict. These confrontations often arose when I attempted to address how his bad behavior affected me and made me feel. The discards were conveniently timed during holidays or planned outings. Whenever I tried to hold him accountable, he'd swiftly play the victim card, saying, "There's no way to please you. Since I can't meet your standards, maybe we should part ways so you can find someone else. It's pointless trying to talk to you." Sometimes, his inner voice would say, "Finish her" in a Mortal Kombat voice, and he would yell, scream, and curse. It became a predictable pattern, leaving me feeling invalidated and dismissed, but I was always prepared for it.

He reacted out of fear and control. He made adjustments when he thought he was about to lose me, and it was short-lived. He would get cocky once I allowed him back. He didn't even give me time to doubt him before he repeated the same reason I left.

The discard could be abrupt, which mine always was, or it can be gradual. In a gradual discard, you will experience withdrawal. They may suddenly become emotionally distant, cold, or indifferent towards you. They may stop communicating, become unresponsive to messages or calls, and withdraw affection or attention.

Next you will experience projection and the blame game in which they may shift blame onto you for the problems in the relationship. They may accuse you of being needy, demanding, or unreasonable, creating a narrative where you are at fault for the breakup.

On the way out, they will devalue you, belittling your worth or importance in their life. They may dismiss your feelings, needs, or concerns, making you feel insignificant or unworthy of love and attention. It's a huge mind screw. They will provide little to no explanation for the breakup, so you can feel confused and abandoned. If confronted, they may provide vague, dismissive responses, but either way, you will be to blame.

The N-word may provide little to no explanation or closure for the breakup, leaving you feeling confused, abandoned, and emotionally devastated. They may ignore attempts at communication or provide vague, dismissive responses when confronted.

Overall, the narcissist's abrupt ending of the relationship or withdrawal of affection during the discarding phase is a deliberate tactic to maintain control and power over you. It also serves to destabilize you emotionally, leaving you vulnerable and dependent on the narcissist for validation, closure, and approval. Because they can't be alone, they already have their replacement squad roster waiting for an opening.

The new supply has already been in the process of being love-bombed and groomed before the discard of you even occurred. The new supply knew all about you before you did them.

One thing a narc is known for, and that is spinning the block, circling back around to you, waiting for holidays to send you that text to initiate contact with you and disrupt your peace when you have your mindset to move on. We call this hoovering.

Think of the Hoover vacuum, a popular brand known for its powerful suction. The term is used figuratively to describe how narcissists "suck" you back into the relationship after a period of discarding or distancing. Just as a vacuum cleaner sucks up dirt and debris from the floor, they use hoovering as a manipulative tactic to draw you back into their dirty world. It's their way of ensuring you're always stuck in their dirt while they stay shiny and clean. They may shower you with affection, promises of change, or declarations of love, creating a sense of false hope and luring you back into the toxic dynamic.

They typically do this when the new supply that came after you is lacking in the supply they're giving him, so they go back to familiar territory for a hit. Because they need continuous supply and thrive on admiration from others, when you leave or distance yourself from the narcissist, it disrupts their source of supply. Hoovering allows the narcissist to regain control over you and secure an additional source of supply.

Another reason they hoover is that they have a deep-seated fear of abandonment and rejection. When their supply leaves after being discarded, it triggers their abandonment wounds and threatens their fragile sense of self-worth. Hoovering allows the narcissist to alleviate their fear of abandonment by reestablishing contact and reasserting control over you. Hoovering also provides a narcissist with an ego boost and a sense of power and superiority. It reaffirms their belief that they are irresistible and all-powerful, capable of manipulating others to do their bidding.

When a narcissist returns after discarding you, it's not because they've had a sudden epiphany and realize how amazing you are. They're not coming back to honor, love, or respect you. Instead, they're circling back to finish what they started. They're returning to trigger you emotionally, not to treat you well. They don't want to treat you right but they don't want you to move on either. They intentionally will try to stay on your good side after abusing you to make it easier to keep tabs on you. It also aids in them having access to you to control you, and to make it appear to outsiders that they must not be that bad if you're still in their good graces. It is not because they miss you, need you, and want you in their lives. Remember, you are there to feed the supply they assigned you to.

Narcissists often reach out when they sense that you are healing and moving forward. They might message, email, call, or text you just to see if they can still manipulate your emotions and maintain their hold over you. It's crucial not to fall prey to this tactic, known as "hoovering," where they try to lure you back with charm, a fake friendship, and false promises.

I encourage you to resist these attempts. Ignore their messages and go without contact and stay no contact. There is nothing positive that can come from reconnecting with them. Instead, you'll likely accumulate more pain. Their return has no positive purpose. It's merely an attempt to disturb your peace and bring chaos back into your life.

Ari wasn't afraid to cry in front of me. He used tears as one of the ways to hoover me. At the time, I thought they were tears of love he felt for me and tears of passion for the relationship, but in retrospect, they were tears of manipulation and tears of internal traumas he was harboring within. He would just let them out when he saw an opportunity.

Narcs often have multiple sources of narcissistic supply, always including past victims. Hoovering allows them to maintain a roster of potential supply sources, ensuring that they always have someone to turn to when their current sources are unavailable or depleted.

When they know you are on to them, the toxic dick you were strong enough to walk away from is now gasping for air. They know you see them for who they are. Their ego is shattered. They will do everything they can to rope you back, and it doesn't matter how long or how much time passes. It can be 2 days or several years. Their aim is to unsettle you and give the impression of remorse. They might even offer apologies or express a desire to make things right. However, it's all meaningless. The narcissist doesn't genuinely care about you or have your best interests at heart. Their sole motive is to secure a source of supply. Perhaps their new supply has caught on to their ways, prompting them to seek a return to the old source. Don't be deceived. Narcissists do not change.

They are almost certain to resurface once you walk away. Their return isn't always about reigniting a romantic relationship. Sometimes, it's just to validate their false sense of importance in your life. Any reaction, whether positive or negative, feeds their ego and sense of significance. They view you as their possession, and they'll return periodically, seeking to reclaim what they believe is theirs. This behavior stems from their disturbed mindset.

Every time you reconcile with a narcissist, their actions escalate. It signals to them that you'll forgive them no matter how poorly they treat you, granting them immunity. Over time, the fake apologies cease. They begin to believe that you deserve the abuse. The cycle of abuse repeats endlessly. Love bombing, devaluation, discard and the hoover. Rinse and repeat. The abuse cycle doesn't alter, it only worsens with each recurrence. Breaking free from this pattern requires you to go no contact. Continuing to endure the abuse only diminishes their respect for you further. They cannot respect someone who allows and tolerates abuse.

My N-word would stop at nothing to lure me back, whether it was tears, food, being extra nice, a small gift, a promise of a trip, you name it, he tried it. I once told him I would consider it if we went to couple's therapy. He declined. I continued to mention it with each hoover attempt, and he continued to decline. Finally, once he realized I was serious, he agreed.

Going to couples therapy with a narcissist is a waste of copay and everyone's time. He manipulated the story, denied my side of the story, and presented himself as a perfect angel. He then got upset when he saw the therapist siding with me and trying to assist him in seeing things through my lens. Trying to resolve a problem with a person who doesn't even think they have is problem is a problem in itself.

We only made it through three sessions because he accused the therapist of taking my side because we are both women. He then got me to agree to stop the therapy and resolve our issues ourselves. He came up with "Watchful Wednesdays." During this time, on Wednesday at 7pm we would have a conversation about our issues. We would rotate weeks, and whoever that Wednesday belonged to, the other couldn't talk but just listen and not judge. Watchful Wednesday turned into Catastrophic Wednesday. When it was my Wednesday to air out my grievances, he would over-talk and argue me down. When it was his Wednesday, he would use it to tell me everything about myself that he didn't like, that didn't exist, to try to shrink my opinion about myself.

I finally said screw Wednesdays and every other day of the week, for that matter and walked away again. He tried to wait it out and I was prepared for the road of healing, but he wouldn't let me be.

Anything Ari could do to get my attention he would. He would intentionally have me leave things at his place and use that as an excuse to reach out to me to see me to return it. It could be something as small as a bobby pin for my hair or a black washcloth for my face. Once he even reached out and asked me what he should do with an old eyelash strip I left there.

I made the error of allowing him back into my life as a friend. It was a significant mistake. We were friends with benefits for well over a year after a 2-year toxic courtship, but I surely wasn't the one who benefited from a thing. Somehow, I felt I could detach from him and heal myself while in this vulnerable position. It seemed like taking two steps forward and one step backwards.

He didn't deserve that much from me, but I figured a slow wean is less drastic than cold turkey. I felt powerless to change my circumstances despite experiencing repeated attempts to regain control or improve my situation. I would continuously ask him if he was involved with anyone, and his response was always, "No, I'm just doing me." Of course, there was supply, but was there anyone meaningful? According to him, there was not. Then, I later found out he was in a full-blown relationship the entire time.

After a year of bad decisions, I finally decided to remove him as a beneficiary but stay in contact. He would always find a reason to reach out to me. He knew I had a soft spot for his dogs so he would use them by asking me to dog sit while he was out of town. He would continuously try my hand and hint at getting back together by sending pictures of us and trying to take a trip down memory lane. He would try to hoover me with food and dick. His weak attempts fell on deaf ears. Once I got a whiff of peace and felt how good it smelled and felt free from stress and toxicity, there was no way I was going back. I love it here.

Even when he tried to play the friend card, his presence still felt like a storm cloud on a sunny day. His presence in my life brought about a lingering uneasiness. I couldn't shake off the feeling of being bound, unable to feel truly liberated. Despite the brighter days, an undercurrent of anxiety surfaced whenever his name flashed on my phone screen. It wasn't me he wanted, it was access to me. It was always him initiating contact, never me. Those constant feelings of uneasiness were a harsh reality that I wasn't fully healed and his continuous attempts at trying to keep me in his life may not be a good idea for me.

Being friends with a narcissist after being in a relationship with them will inevitably lead to trouble. I found myself still entangled in his web of control, unable to break free. I still felt the eggshells beneath my feet when we spoke. When a narcissist claims they want to be friends but not in a romantic relationship, it's just another tactic to manipulate and exploit you. It's an ego boost that they're still able to get a response from you. You are simply just a secondary source of supply.

They'll demand unreasonable favors, guilt-trip you if you refuse, and label you a bad friend. This is precisely why they're no longer with you. They're seeking to use you in different ways. They may intentionally treat you as a friend with benefits, ensuring you never move on and remain emotionally attached. You cannot maintain a healthy friendship with a narcissist because their goal is to keep you on the hook and prevent you from happily moving on with someone else while they are out doing them. A narcissist doesn't deserve your grace or your friendship. Stop being a blessing to them and instead be the lesson they need to learn. Invoice them for that karmic debt they owe.

I developed a learned helplessness. All that did was enable my dependency on the narcissist for validation and stability, further reinforcing the power imbalance in the relationship even though we were no longer together.

He was always kind to anyone who took his side but waged war against those who didn't. Over time, others began to see through his façade, even members of his own family. His treatment of his sibling was appalling. Shortly after the untimely passing of his beloved mother, around her birthday, instead of offering care and consolation, he reeked havoc over the estate, and he sent a text to his sibling taunting her stating that he was their mom's favorite. It was a cruel, self-serving act, characteristic of his inability to empathize, even in moments of shared grief. It was also a clear projection of his insecurities, deliberately aimed to hurt her during a time of mourning. Deep down, he likely felt like the less favored and lashed out in an attempt to mask his own feelings of inadequacy.

One day, I came across a revealing social media post from one of his relatives, acknowledging the presence of narcissistic behavior within their family. When I commented on the post, expressing my familiarity with such behavior, he immediately reached out, demanding that I delete my comment.

True to narcissistic form, the "hollering hit dog" lashed out, attempting to manipulate me. He disparaged the family member in question, labeling her an opportunist and insincere, and even launched a smear campaign against her, trying to rally others to his side. He pressured me to choose between them, but knowing the genuine and kind-hearted nature of his family member, someone I considered a friend, I stood by her. That decision was the final straw for him. He never reached out to me again, and I can't begin to describe how liberating that was. The sun has shined brighter every day since, even on the rainiest of days.

One thing about a narcissist, when they lose control over you, they go all out to control what other people think of you. This incident provided me with the clarity and resolve I needed to break free.

While the discard and hoover phases of a toxic relationship with a narcissist can be incredibly challenging and painful, they also mark significant milestones on the journey to healing and liberation. By recognizing the manipulation tactics at play, setting boundaries, and prioritizing self-care, individuals can reclaim their power and break free from the grip of toxicity. Remember, you are not alone on this journey. With perseverance, self-compassion, and support from others, you can emerge stronger, wiser, and ready to embrace a life of authenticity and fulfillment. The road ahead may be daunting, but it is also filled with endless possibilities for growth, resilience, and healing. Keep moving forward, for brighter days are on the horizon. Remember, a narcissist's rejection is your protection!

CHAPTER 10:
TRAUMA BONDS – THE INVISIBLE CHAINS

"I got so comfortable with being miserable that I forgot peace and happiness was an option"

Alright, time to dive deep, so stay with me. Let's talk about the physiological standpoint of a trauma bond. When narcissists pull their love-bombing BS, they're basically turning you into their science project and conditioning you. They flood your system with feel-good chemicals like endorphins and dopamine, giving you a euphoric high that's better than a Venti cold foam triple espresso with multiple pumps of vanilla. But when the love bombing stops, they switch gears to manipulation, spiking your cortisol levels and sending you into stressful fight or flight mode. This emotional rollercoaster keeps your body swinging like a pendulum between bliss and panic. This is called a peptide addiction. While both peptide addiction and trauma bonding play a role in unhealthy relationships, they operate at different levels. Peptide addiction is biological, and the trauma bond is psychological/emotional.

Peptide addiction helps explain why people feel stuck in toxic relationships and develop trauma bonds. In abusive relationships, the constant ups and downs, moments of love and kindness followed by hurt and rejection cause the brain to release chemicals, called peptides, linked to those emotions. Over time, the body gets used to this cycle and starts craving those emotional highs and lows, even though they're harmful. This is similar to trauma bonding, where the victim feels deeply attached to their abuser despite the pain they cause. The abuser's mix of affection and cruelty strengthens this connection, making it hard to leave.

Understanding peptide addiction shows that breaking free isn't just emotional, it's also about letting the body and brain recover from this unhealthy cycle. These toxic masterminds have you pegged. They've done their homework. That's why their intoxicating high is so hard to replicate. Your body starts craving that rush, making you feel inexplicably tied to them. This hormonal seesaw tricks your system into thinking you need them to survive. Even though they make you feel awful, escaping their grip feels next to impossible. And voila, that's how a trauma bond forms.

Narcissists are like emotional pendulums, swinging wildly between Dr. Jekyll and Mr. Hyde. One moment, they're showering you with kindness, and the next, they're as mean as an untrained rabid pit bull. This back-and-forth is enough to make anyone's head spin. It's tough to know if they're genuinely good or just putting on a show. Often, you cling to the hope that the good side is their true self, ignoring the red flags because it's too heartbreaking to admit the truth about someone you care about but we often become color blind because those red flags turn green.

But here's the kicker, over time, the scales tip, and you start seeing more of Mr. Hyde than Dr. Jekyll. Sometimes, their "good" behavior is just them hitting the pause button on their abuse. You end up clinging to those brief moments of peace, mistaking them for the real deal.

An easy way to spot a trauma bond? When you can't stand them, they're ruining your happiness and health, yet you still can't let go. You're stuck in a loop of misery, hoping for the next fleeting glimpse of their better side.

A trauma bond occurs when someone becomes emotionally attached to a toxic individual due to the intense experiences they've shared, typically involving abuse or trauma. To keep it simple, A trauma bond is a deep emotional connection that forms between a person and someone who abuses or mistreats them. When you are trauma-bonded, YOU TRY TO CONVINCE THE PERSON WHO IS HURTING YOU TO TREAT YOU BETTER INSTEAD OF WALKING AWAY.

One of the key components of trauma bonding is intermittent reinforcement. This occurs when the toxic individual alternates between kindness and cruelty, creating a cycle of hope and despair. For instance, an abusive partner may shower you with affection and apologies after an episode of violence, leading you to believe that they will change.

Trauma-bonded individuals can also experience Stockholm Syndrome. Stockholm Syndrome is a specific form of trauma bonding that occurs when hostages develop positive feelings toward their captors. This can happen in abusive relationships as well, where the victim empathizes with the abuser and may even defend them against others. Think of it like when your captor's charm becomes your defense mechanism, and you start rooting for the villain in your own life's movie. You start making excuses for your partner's toxic behavior, convincing yourself that they're just misunderstood or going through a rough patch.

Those who are trauma-bonded often become emotionally dependent on their partners for validation, approval, and a sense of identity. This dependency can make it difficult for you to leave the relationship, even when they recognize it's harmful.

Trauma bonding is often reinforced by the cycle of abuse, which typically consists of tension building, explosion, reconciliation, and calm. You may cling to the moments of reconciliation and hope for change despite the ongoing abuse.

One can often experience cognitive dissonance, where they hold contradictory beliefs about the narcissist and the relationship. On one hand, they may recognize the abuse and want to leave, but on the other hand, they may feel a deep emotional attachment to their abuser and fear the consequences of leaving.

In some cases, trauma bonding can be seen as a survival mechanism, as one may believe that staying with the narcissist is safer than leaving or confronting them. This is particularly common in situations where one fears retaliation or further harm if they try to escape.

In a trauma bond, a negative and dysfunctional attachment takes place, compelling you to remain despite enduring abuse, shame, misery, and criticism. There are a few distinct ways to detect if you are in a toxic relationship and if your actions are at risk for being in a trauma bond.

One way is if the relationship is consistently unpredictable. For instance, if a partner alternates between being affectionate and loving one moment and demeaning and hurtful the next, they may shower you with gifts and compliments one day only to criticize and belittle you the next.

When you desperately want to leave but can't, it is another sign you are trauma bonded. They will give you unpredictable reactions and you find yourself walking on eggshells around them, never knowing how they will react to different situations. For example, a small disagreement may escalate into a full-blown argument or even physical violence without warning.

If they disrespect or betray you, you constantly give them multiple chances. When you let them get away with things they should be apologizing for, yet you are justifying their actions in your head. Those are prime examples that you are in an unhealthy attachment.

Another way to determine if you are in a toxic relationship is if you feel responsible for their happiness, putting yourself in a position of conditional affection. The narc may only show affection or approval when you comply with their demands or meet their expectations. As a result, you learn to associate your own worth and value with your ability to please them, reinforcing the belief that you are responsible for their happiness. You end up expecting and fearing negative consequences or retaliation if you fail to meet their expectations or make them unhappy. This fear can be amplified by past experiences leading you to prioritize their happiness over your own well-being. Your sense of responsibility for their happiness is often rooted in manipulation, fear, empathy, and a distorted sense of duty. Breaking free from this requires challenging these dynamics and recognizing that you are not responsible for the abuser's emotions or behavior.

When you defend the relationship and feel it's impossible to leave knowing you're unhappy, and it's mentally abusive, and you miss them a great deal when they're gone despite the treatment you received, it is also a sign you're in a toxic situation and a manipulative bond.

Another key component of a trauma bond is Euphoric recall. Euphoric recall can reinforce and perpetuate the trauma bond by romanticizing or idealizing the relationship, making it harder to recognize the toxicity or leave the abusive situation. The positive memories and emotional highs experienced during euphoric recall strengthened the emotional attachment to him despite the negative consequences of the relationship.

First off, our brains tend to focus on positive memories while downplaying or even ignoring negative ones. In a toxic relationship, this means we might excessively remember the good times, the laughter, affection, and happy moments, while glossing over or rationalizing away the pain, arguments, and mistreatment.

Secondly, toxic relationships often involve cycles of abuse followed by periods of remorse, love bombing, or genuine affection from the abuser. These intermittent "highs" can create a sense of euphoria or relief, reinforcing the positive memories and making it harder to acknowledge or leave behind the toxic aspects of the relationship.

Ultimately, euphoric recall serves as a coping mechanism, helping us cope with the confusion of being in a toxic relationship by focusing on the moments of happiness and hope while downplaying or rationalizing away the pain and dysfunction.

In essence, euphoric recall and a trauma bond work together to keep individuals trapped in toxic relationships as they cling to the fleeting moments of happiness and hope while enduring the pain and turmoil inflicted by their abuser. Recognizing and addressing both experiences is crucial for breaking free from the cycle of abuse and reclaiming one's well-being.

Another way is when the joy of being in a relationship has been replaced with a strong fear of losing it. In a healthy relationship, things shouldn't occur for you to have this fear lingering in the back of your mind. When that feeling of excitement has turned into sadness, anxiety, and the feeling of desperation, you may need to reevaluate things and take a closer look into what is causing these feelings of uneasiness.

If your mood depends on the state of the relationship, you are rapidly heading down the path of a toxic attachment. When your mood is consistently tied to the state of your relationship, it indicates a deep emotional dependence and vulnerability, characteristic of a trauma bond. Your emotional well-being becomes contingent upon your partner's approval, validation, and behavior, creating a cycle of dependency and instability.

When a relationship is characterized by extreme highs and lows, it often indicates the presence of a trauma bond. The imbalance between intense affection and conflict creates an emotional rollercoaster that can be deeply destabilizing and addictive. Extreme highs, such as moments of love bombing or intense passion, may create an intense emotional attachment to the partner, while the lows, marked by manipulation or gaslighting, create feelings of dependence and fear. This cycle of intense emotions forms the basis of a trauma bond, where you become psychologically entangled with them despite recognizing the harmful nature of the relationship.

Another way to recognize when things are emotionally abusive is when you are uncertain about the relationship a majority of the time but dread losing it because you're happy some of the time. When you find yourself constantly oscillating between uncertainty about the relationship and the fear of losing it while clinging to the fleeting moments of happiness, it's a clear sign that an unhealthy attachment is forming. This inconsistency arises from the intense emotional rollercoaster rides, characteristic of toxic relationships, where fleeting moments of joy or affection become amplified and cherished in contrast to feelings of instability, fear, and doubt. Not recognizing the toxicity and unpredictability of the relationship, the fear of losing intermittent positive experiences creates a powerful attachment to them, perpetuating the cycle of a codependent dynamic.

Obsessively analyzing every aspect of the relationship, constantly trying to decipher its complexities and make sense of the narc's behavior, is another strong indicator. You will often feel compelled to rationalize or justify their actions, hoping to uncover a solution or pattern that will restore stability and security to the relationship.

If you find yourself constantly walking on eggshells, fearing criticism, and feeling the need to justify or explain yourself at every turn, it's a clear indication that you're in a toxic situation. In such relationships, you experience being controlled through intimidation, manipulation, and constant scrutiny of your actions. This creates an atmosphere of fear, self-doubt, and insecurity, where you, the victim, feels constantly on edge and unable to express yourself freely without facing judgment or retaliation, making it difficult for you to assert your own needs and boundaries.

I used to gloat about this connection that I had with my narcissistic ex, not understanding that a trauma bond is also a form of a connection. The toxicity was at an all-time high. Our connection was toxic, not beautiful. I was a prisoner of war.

His triggers triggered my triggers. His abandonment issues fed into my codependency that I mistook for a "bond." I would tell myself it's love, but let's be real, it was more like an addiction we couldn't shake. I was stuck in a trap disguised as a romance. The narcissistic knot was impossible to untangle.

Over and over, I would convince myself things were getting better, but the truth is that I was learning to tolerate the toxicity. Toxic was my new normal. I was heavily trauma bonded. I was willing to stay under the worst conditions. And after being discarded, I was willing to go back under the most humiliating terms. What I learned is that the longer you stay, the more you overlook, and the worse it gets.

Recognizing emotionally abusive relationships is also understanding what a healthy relationship looks like. In a healthy relationship, both partners respect each other's boundaries, opinions, and autonomy. There is a sense of equality and mutual appreciation for each other's strengths and weaknesses. Healthy individuals take care of things they want to keep.

I was living in a blissful cocoon of ignorance. I chose to only face the truth that made me happy and not the ugly truth. My toxic relationship had me in a chokehold. A relationship with a healthy individual should never cause strife, fear, and anxiousness. I literally felt like I was suffocating. My daily life seemed like a constant back-and-forth roller coaster ride. It literally had me crashing out where an escape felt like an impossible feat, and every attempt to break free only tightened the grip further.

Healthy relationships thrive on open, honest, respectful and effective communication. Partners feel comfortable expressing their thoughts, feelings, and needs and actively listen to each other without judgment.

Trust is the foundation of a healthy relationship. Partners support each other's goals and aspirations and trust each other to be faithful, reliable, and honest.

Healthy relationships are also characterized by emotional intimacy, where partners feel safe and secure sharing their deepest thoughts, fears, and desires. There is a strong emotional connection and sense of intimacy that deepens over time.

Disagreements and conflicts are inevitable in any relationship, but in a healthy relationship, partners work together to resolve conflicts constructively and respectfully. They communicate openly, seek compromise, and prioritize finding solutions that benefit both parties.

None of this was present in my relationship. With toxicity and negativity being at the forefront of my relationship, I was never reminded of what a healthy relationship felt like.

I tried to leave him more times than I could count, but every attempt seemed to only make his hold on me tighter. One night I felt extremely exhausted and defeated. We argued. He yelled. And I told him to leave my house and never come back. I sat on the cold tile floor of my bathroom, hugging my knees pulled to my chest, rocking back and forth slowly staring blankly at the door he had slammed on his way out because he was upset that I corrected him about a feature on the Iphone.

But then, the phone rings. It's always him. His voice, calm and full of that false sweetness, slips through the crack in my defenses. "I need you," he'll say, or "I can't live without you." And somehow, even after everything he's done, I find myself walking back into the mess, into his chaos, into his control.

I know what he is. I know that his love is a weapon that is just a tool he uses to keep me tangled in his world. One minute, he's cold, distant, barely acknowledging me, and the next, he's pouring on the affection, making me feel like I'm the only person that matters.

I've heard all the advice from friends, from people who care about me. They've told me to leave, to walk away for good. But how do I explain to them that when I try, it feels like something inside me is pulling back? His cruelty and kindness are like two sides of the same coin, and I'm stuck in the middle, spinning between them, unsure of what's real anymore.

I've done everything they told me to do. I've gone no-contact, I've walked away with every ounce of strength I thought I had left, but nothing ever worked. I always found myself coming back, even though I knew, deep down, it was destroying me. His presence is like a drug, and I'm addicted. No matter how much it tears me apart, there's a part of me that craves it, that believes if I just hold on a little longer, maybe this time he'll finally be the man I want him to be.

But tonight, something is different. My phone buzzes again. His name flashes across the screen, and I can feel my chest tighten with that familiar rush of panic. But instead of answering, I just sit there, frozen for a second. Then something inside of me breaks free.

I finally *see* him for what he is. A manipulator. A liar. Someone who has drained every ounce of my self-worth and made me believe it was my fault. The chains are still there, I can feel them, but for the first time, they don't seem so heavy. I'm not broken. I'm not what he's made me believe.

I stand up, my legs shaking, but my mind is clearer than it's ever been. I'm afraid, but there's something else that I haven't felt in a long time. Hope. I know I have to do the work, but I also know that I'm stronger than I thought.

This time, I'm really leaving. At that moment, I had reached the point where I would rather mop the ocean with a Q-Tip, sweep the sand on a beach with a toothbrush, and spell out 'Never Again' in the sand with a chopstick before I ever consider going back or entering another toxic situation. I don't know what will happen next, but I'm never going back.

FOUR

FROM GASLIGHT TO DAYLIGHT

CHAPTER 11:
MOVING ON – LET GO, FORGIVE YOURSELF FIRST

"Let it hurt, let it bleed, let it heal, let it go"
-Nikita Gill

I had a day of retail therapy Saturday at the mall after a long morning cleaning out my closet. I planned to partake in some shopping, get my nails done, grab some bras at Victoria's Secret, and grab a sweet treat and smoothie for dinner. The mall food court was packed and smelled of freshly baked pizza and bourbon chicken with fried rice. After accepting free samples of sesame chicken pretending to have interest in ordering a plate, I decided I would grab a seat to enjoy my Caramel cinnamon roll and smoothie. Many seats were full, so I set my bags on the chair next to me and sat next to two middle aged women in front of the Panda Express. I was ear-hustling at the two of them having a deep conversation. One woman was discussing how unhappy she was in her marriage and how abusive her husband is, yet she wasn't quite ready to leave and destroy their family.

I pretended like I wasn't listening, yet I was heavily invested, saving the center of the cinnamon roll for the juicy part of the story. In true good girlfriend fashion, the woman was pouring heavily into her friend, giving her advice. She said, "The best way to kill something is to let it starve. No action. No response. No altercation. Just don't feed it. That's where the true power lies." I could have choked on my cinnamon roll right there on the spot. I immediately wrote it down in the notes section of my phone because I knew I would end up referencing it at some point. That is exactly what happens to a narcissist when you cut off their supply. They starve.

The next morning, I decided that I was going to church. I needed clarity, a sign, something to shake me out of the fog that had been clouding my mind. As I settled into my seat, the sweet tones of the chorus filled the room, but it was the pastor's words that struck like lightning.

His sermon seemed to be aimed straight at my soul, as though he had peeked into my life and saw the mess I was trying to hold together. "Your ability to soar and take off is tied to what you are willing to take off," he declared, his voice firm yet compassionate. "Elimination leads to elevation. A plane cannot take off if it's weighed down with too much baggage. And if it tries, it could crash. God wants you to grow, but you can't soar while clinging to what's holding you back. What you're crying over is stopping you from crossing over." "Endings," he said, with his voice rising, "are entrances into new seasons."

Each word pierced me deeper. The weight I'd been carrying suddenly felt tangible, an anchor I'd been dragging for far too long. His words were a lifeline, pulling me towards something I hadn't yet named but desperately needed. Normally, I'd sit still, blending into the congregation like a shadow, but this time, I couldn't stay silent. Before I knew it, I was on my feet, shouting, "Yes sir, PREACH!" My voice rang out, surprising even me, but I meant every syllable.

The message clicked. I realized in that moment that the life I wanted, the growth I craved, was on the other side of the very things I was refusing to let go of. The minute I truly committed to releasing those burdens, my life began to flourish in ways I hadn't even known were possible. Areas of my soul that had been parched for years were suddenly blooming and hydrated. It was as though God had been waiting for me to finally shed the weight so he could show me the path forward.

Breaking up with a narcissist? It's like exiting a circus where the clowns have taken over the entire show. Picture this: you're saying farewell to a relationship that's been a rollercoaster of gaslighting, manipulation, lies, and the occasional side order of cheating. Your self-esteem? It's taken a sabbatical, leaving you feeling like you're walking a tightrope. You're a cocktail of emotional anxiety, a splash of hurt, a smidgen of anger, with a generous twist of "What the hell just happened?"

But wait, there's more! Closure? Validation? Tuh, you'd have better luck finding a vegan at a butcher shop. The narcissist? Humph, they're unbothered and living their best life. What about your heartache? Your vulnerability? They will literally have no damns to give you.

So, here you are, feeling like the star of a twisted reality show or soap opera (depending on your age), grieving a character who vanished quicker than free shrimp at a hood wedding reception. And to top it all off, your support squad, bless their hearts, might not quite get the complexity of it all or be able to offer you the proper words of advice.

There was a time when I never thought I would have my N-word out of my life. He felt it necessary to stick around using any excuse or holiday to keep in touch, and I felt it necessary to allow him. It wasn't until I realized his absence brought me peace and that I didn't lose him, but I regained a better version of myself. My record with good men was damn near impeccable. To this day, there was never any animosity or friction with anyone I was involved with. What I wasn't going to do was to be that woman who built him up for the next woman while he damaged me for the next man.

I felt like I had only two options. Was I going to chase the dream or embrace the nightmare? Leaving didn't seem possible. I thought that leaving would break my heart. Leaving won't break your heart. It will heal your spirit. Let me repeat that. Leaving won't break your heart. It will heal your spirit. But the clutches of a trauma bond will make leaving seem impossible, so mentally, you will tend to accept and adjust because the thought of leaving weighs heavier than staying and taking the abuse. After all, there would be some good and happy times to cling to, right? Wrong.

Trying to leave seems impossible because the minute you're ready, the person you always hoped for them to be shows up. I've been through the cycle so much that I knew it was temporary, so I knew better this time. I always said that God had a sense of humor. It was like I could hear him say, "Baby girl, I tried showing you who he was, but you didn't trust me, so check this out." And something worse would happen.

Things would never change. Struggling with setting boundaries, he remained in my life, but I had kept him at arm's length. That helped me, but it didn't heal me. I finally pulled up my big girl panties and decided I had enough. I was done. I learned not to try to keep the same people around me that I needed to heal from.

How did I do it? Two words. No contact. No contact means refraining from all forms of communication with the toxic person, including phone calls, text messages, emails, social media interactions, and in-person meetings. It involves blocking the person's phone number, email address, and social media profiles to prevent any attempts at contact. It is a way of enforcing personal boundaries and protecting yourself from further harm. It sends a clear message to them that their behavior is unacceptable and that any attempts to reach out will not be tolerated.

It was important that I provided a space to focus on my healing and well-being without interference. Even though I tried to do this by being just friends with him, it was still an entryway to the cycle of manipulation, control, and abuse. I knew keeping him around would stunt the process of healing and recovery.

Because the process was gradual, it didn't have a major effect on me as being discarded did. As you come to terms with the end of the relationship, you may experience sadness and a sense of loss. You may mourn the person you thought your partner was or the dreams and expectations you had for the relationship. You mentally go through the stages of grief. Initially, there may be a sense of disbelief and denial, especially if the relationship ended abruptly or unexpectedly. You might find yourself questioning whether the relationship was truly toxic or if there was something you could have done differently to salvage it.

As the reality of its ending sank in, I experienced intense feelings of resentment and anger toward him and even toward myself for allowing the relationship to continue for as long as it did. I felt resentful about the ways in which I was mistreated or manipulated.

Guilt then came into play, and I found myself replaying events in my mind, wondering if there was something I could have done to change the outcome of the relationship. I mainly experienced feelings of guilt for not leaving sooner and for allowing myself to be treated poorly. I've never been a fool or sucker for love. I felt a certain way because I got caught slipping.

With time and self-reflection, I began to accept the reality of the situation and was very comfortable about letting it go. I gained clarity about the unhealthy dynamics that existed and recognized that ending the relationship was the best decision for my overall well-being. I felt a huge sense of empowerment and a renewed focus on self-care and personal growth.

Once my healing was in motion, I realized how much I had taken myself for granted. The longer I stayed, the less I loved myself. The minute I left, the more I valued myself. My appearance even improved. Blemishes I had on my skin went away. The headaches I once had disappeared. My blood pressure normalized. I started eating better and exercising. My appetite for better things surfaced. I gained happy weight. The sense of panic diminished, and each day, he became a distant memory.

I asked myself several times what was wrong with me to even tolerate it? Was it the fear of starting over? Was it my inability to think for myself because my mind was taken over by someone else? Was it that I felt it was easier to try to fix someone rather than get to know someone new? Was it the hesitation of coming across another narcissist when my current narcissist was familiar to me? Looking back, I think it was a combination of all those things.

The journey was difficult. I took a break from dating and prayed, I purged, I read books, I dove into my business, I wrote affirmations, hung out more with friends, traveled, submerged myself with work, journaled my feelings from the relationship, and yet I still felt like one foot was stuck in the mud.

I finally realized that the key to me moving forward in a much healthier way that was not currently a part of my healing process was the F-word. Not the four-letter one you are thinking of. The word I am speaking of is forgiveness. Some Christians may feel conflicted about this perspective, as forgiveness is often seen as a spiritual mandate. However, forgiveness, like love, is deeply personal and must come from a place of authenticity, not obligation. Forgiving someone who harmed you is not a pre-requisite for peace and healing. Choosing not to forgive them until you are ready, on your own time, is okay.

You do not need to immediately sacrifice your soul on the altar of forgiveness for someone who betrayed you thinking that it's the fast-track path for peace. Peace is not found in pardoning those who hurt you, it is found in protecting yourself from further harm. Forgiving them while still vulnerable will not heal you. It may only invite them to wound you again. Forgiveness, as God teaches, begins with the heart. The forgiveness that should take priority is your own. I believe you need to forgive yourself before you can forgive someone else.

Forgive yourself for the moments you stayed silent, for the times you ignored the red flags, and for every time you gave them another chance. Forgive yourself for the mistakes you made when you didn't know any better. Forgive yourself for trusting, for hoping, for enduring when they didn't deserve you.

Forgive yourself for staying in a toxic relationship for too long knowing damn well you should have left after the first red flag. Forgive yourself for blaming yourself for problems you never caused just to appease another person to keep them close. Forgive yourself for loving someone who couldn't love you back, for giving endlessly when you received nothing in return, and for letting your worth be defined by someone who didn't see it.

Take accountability, forgive yourself completely—and set yourself free.

Forgiving yourself for staying in a toxic relationship for an extended period can be a challenging but crucial part of your healing journey. Aside from seeking forgiveness from myself, I had to ask God to forgive me for ignoring the signs he was sending me over and over and for losing the beautiful, strong woman he created. I had to relearn to love myself more than I hated him.

I had to own my part in the experience because I ignored all the signs and disregarded my own intuition. I had to give myself permission to recognize and embrace the emotions that surfaced when I reflected on my past choices. The feelings of stupidity, regret, shame, guilt, embarrassment, or anger continued to haunt me. I finally understood that experiencing a variety of emotions is natural, and it's important to allow yourself to feel them without criticism or judgment. It was nice to start to see the quiet watered-down version of myself leaving and the happy free-spirited version returning.

One thing I had to do was be mindful of any negative self-talk or self-blame that arose. I had to replace those thoughts with compassionate and empowering statements. I had to remind myself that I am capable and worthy of forgiveness and deserving of love and compassion, both from myself and from others. I also had to give myself the proverbial flowers and remember my value even when I didn't receive back the love I gave and deserved. I would pat myself on the back and stop dwelling on past mistakes to recognize the lessons and growth that have come from my experiences. I had to remind myself I had something to be proud of and acknowledge the strengths and resilience I've demonstrated in navigating a challenging situation. I had to repeatedly empower myself.

After enduring too much time dealing with manipulation and emotional abuse, it was poetic justice when I found true happiness and self-worth on my own. The more I thrived and embraced my independence, the more it highlighted his failures and insecurities. When you forgive yourself, you reclaim your personal power and agency. It allows you to acknowledge and process painful emotions without getting stuck in a cycle of resentment or self-recrimination, forcing you to recognize that you can shape your own narrative and make choices that align with your values and well-being. This sense of empowerment is very liberating, especially in comparison to the shackles you were in while wallowing in the pits of toxicity.

You will start to realize that finding forgiveness within disrupts the cycle of self-doubt by re-affirming your value and resilience. Not only does it open the door to growth and transformation, but it also invites you to learn from your experiences, cultivate wisdom, and make empowered choices moving forward. By letting go of the past and embracing self-forgiveness, you create space for new opportunities, relationships, and possibilities to emerge and evolve.

Letting go of a toxic relationship is like that famous monkey trap story but with more emotional baggage and fewer bananas. In parts of the world, hunters used a simple but genius method. They'd put fruit inside a jar with a narrow opening. The monkey would reach in, grab the fruit, and boom, its hand got stuck. Here's the kicker, the monkey could free itself at any moment by letting go of the fruit, but it wouldn't. That fruit seemed too good, too worth it, too close to give up. Sound familiar? Toxic relationships work the same way. We hold on, convinced we're about to win something worthwhile, but all we're doing is keeping ourselves trapped.

Here's where it gets real, letting go isn't easy, and the monkey's struggle shows us why. That little fruit looks like everything: validation, affection, the "potential" you believe in so deeply. The monkey isn't stupid, it's just unwilling to believe that the cost of holding on is greater than the value of what it's clinging to. You've probably been there, thinking, "If I just try harder, if I love more, if I wait a little longer, things will change." But let's face it, toxic people are experts at dangling that bait just close enough to keep you hooked.

The truth is, holding on doesn't change them, it traps you. Let me say it louder for the people in the back. Holding on doesn't change them, it traps you. Like the monkey, you'll stay stuck until you realize that freedom is worth more than any crumb they're offering. The monkey probably didn't care if the fruit was bad, he just wanted it and couldn't let it go even though he was aware he could free himself.

Letting go isn't about giving up, it's about reclaiming your life. Sure, the jar might feel safe because it's what you know, but real freedom is out there, waiting for you to be brave enough to release what's holding you back. Drop the bait. Yes, it's hard and your brain will scream, "What if this is as good as it gets?" But the second you let go, you'll see how much bigger and better the world is outside that jar.

So, here's the bottom line: don't let the fear of loss keep you trapped. The monkey learns the hard way that holding on doesn't lead to happiness, it leads to capture. You don't have to make the same mistake. Let go of the toxic person, the false promises, and the never-ending drama. Stop playing tug-of-war with someone who's not even on your team. Freedom is just a decision away, and trust me, it feels a hell of a lot better than being stuck with your hand in someone else's mess. Once you let go, you'll realize the only thing trapping you is your own grip. Let go, boss up, and watch how fast your world changes.

Whatever you are not changing, you are choosing. One more time. WHATVER YOU ARE NOT CHANGING, YOU ARE CHOOSING. This statement is a powerful reminder of the control we have over our lives, even when it doesn't feel like it. Every situation we allow to continue whether it's a toxic relationship, an unfulfilling job, or a destructive habit is a choice. By not addressing what needs to change, we are silently deciding to let it remain as it is.

Bad choices, whether deliberate or by default, have a way of becoming heavy burdens over time. They linger in our minds, weigh on our hearts, and drain our energy. These choices manifest as regret, self-doubt, or the nagging feeling of being stuck. The truth is, what we refuse to confront will continue to confront us, growing larger and harder to ignore.

Change can be uncomfortable, but so is the weight of staying stuck. The longer you avoid change, the heavier that weight becomes. Choosing to act, even in small ways, is the key to breaking free from the patterns that hold you back. You don't have to overhaul your entire life overnight, change begins with a single decision, repeated overtime.

Carrying the weight of bad choices for years is far heavier than the temporary discomfort of taking action. Choosing to change, whether it's setting boundaries, leaving a toxic situation, or pursuing a healthier path, lightens that burden and paves the way for growth, freedom, and peace.

Every small step toward change is a choice to reclaim your life, redefine your story, and honor your worth. So, ask yourself: What am I tolerating in my life right now? And is it time to choose something different?

The choices we make today will define the weight, or the lightness, we carry tomorrow. So be easy on yourself, be patient with yourself and trust that you are deserving of love, forgiveness, and a brighter future. Embrace your grace. Stand in your light and your power and protect your energy. Let go, forgive, and flourish.

CHAPTER 12:
TURNING THE PAGE - PAIN INTO PURPOSE

"I lost myself when I was groomed to accept the bare minimum. I found myself when I rediscovered my worth."

Going no contact and forgiving yourself are huge steps in the healing process, but it's normal to have thoughts of reaching out and to experience regrets. Remember, you were addicted to another person, bound by trauma, so it won't be easy. You're constantly feeling broken, like the ice cream machine at McDonald's.

Breaking free from a narcissist's control can feel like an endless tug-of-war, where every interaction pulls you deeper into their web. But there comes a moment, a turning point, when you realize the balance is shifting. Their usual tricks don't land as hard, their manipulations feel predictable, and your own sense of strength is starting to grow. If you're noticing a change in how you respond to their tactics, you may be closer to winning this battle more than you think. Here are the top 4 signs that you're starting to reclaim your power from a narcissist.

#1: Emotional Detachment

You know you're gaining the upper hand when their tactics start to lose their grip on you. The narcissist's go-to moves: gaslighting, manipulation, attempts to provoke a reaction, just don't pack the same punch. You're less reactive, more centered, and no longer taking their bait. Their words and actions now feel less like arrows and more like annoying background noise.

#2: You Don't Even Bother to Engage

Winning against a narcissist means knowing when *not* to engage. Instead of jumping into their endless power struggles or defending yourself against unfounded accusations, you step back. You choose inner peace over proving a point, refusing to participate in the drama. The argument no longer seems worth it, and you see that real strength lies in walking away.

#3: You See Through Their Game

When you start recognizing the narcissist's patterns and strategies, it's like putting on a pair of glasses that make all their tricks visible. The mind games they used to play. You've got their number now. You see through their tactics as they unfold, and their attempts to manipulate just don't land the way they used to. The more predictable they become, the less effective they are.

#4: You Focus on Self-Care

Instead of pouring energy into dealing with the narcissist, you're redirecting that energy inward. Self-care and self-love have become your priorities as you work on healing and building yourself up. With every step toward recovery, you're reclaiming your time and energy. Seeking support and focusing on your own growth are clear signs you're no longer under the narcissist's spell. You're too busy thriving to worry about their next move.

Getting a toxic person out of your head is like quitting junk food. You know it's bad for you, but somehow you still crave it. The trick? Go on a mental detox. First, remind yourself daily that he's more "expired sour milk" than fine wine. Fill your time with things that make you feel fabulous and don't leave space for his nonsense. And whenever those thoughts creep in, remember you can't miss something that wasn't worth having in the first place.

Healing is like kicking a bad habit. Think about detoxing from alcohol or a social media cleanse. Just like battling an addiction, relapses are a risk, so you'll need some upkeep. This could mean meditating, praying, indulging in self-care, working out, getting therapy, or even a daring new haircut. Participate in whatever keeps you focused on your well-being.

Remember, healing isn't a straight line. Setbacks are part of the ride. To keep yourself motivated, celebrate every tiny win. Each step forward, every moment of clarity, and each act of self-love is a victory worth throwing a mini party for. By sticking to these good habits and treating yourself, you'll keep moving toward real recovery and lasting happiness.

Focus on rebuilding your life and discovering who you are outside that toxic mess. Pour your energy into chasing your goals, passions, and hobbies. Surround yourself with positive vibes and growth opportunities. Don't hesitate to seek therapy if you're feeling stuck or overwhelmed. A pro can offer the guidance and support you need to navigate this tricky time.

Take time to reflect on the lessons learned from the toxic relationship. Consider how the experience has shaped you, what you've discovered about yourself and others, and how you want to learn and grow from it. Use your pain as a catalyst for self-awareness and personal growth. Every hardship contains a lesson, and every lesson contributes to your journey of becoming stronger and more resilient.

Surround yourself with supportive friends, family members, or a therapist who can offer empathy, understanding, and encouragement as you navigate your healing journey. Sharing your experiences with others can help you feel less isolated and validate your feelings. Reconnect with your inner self and rediscover your passions, interests, and values. Invest time and energy into activities that bring you joy, fulfillment, and a sense of purpose. Make sure your cut-off game is strong.

Your healing path will look different and may be shorter or longer than someone else's. Do not compare your journey to anyone else's. My healing path was somewhat short because I was working on detaching while I was attached. I was working on being free while imprisoned.

During the road to healing and regaining yourself, focus on nurturing your physical, emotional, and spiritual well-being. Whether through exercise, meditation, hobbies, or simply spending time with loved ones, prioritize what makes you feel whole and happy. Doing so heals and lays the foundation for a brighter, more fulfilling future.

I used my experience as fuel to drive positive changes in my life and others. I channeled my energy into meaningful pursuits, such as advocacy, public speaking, and creative expression. I wanted to turn my pain into a purpose and as a vessel for helping others who may be going through similar experiences.

It's important to note that grief is a highly individual process, and there is no "right" or "wrong" way to grieve the end of a relationship. You may move through these stages in a different order, experience them multiple times, or find that certain stages are more intense or prolonged than others. It's also normal to experience a range of emotions, including sadness, anger, confusion, and relief, as you navigate the aftermath of a breakup. Allow yourself to feel whatever emotions arise.

Your healing and growth will come in stages and phases. Trust the process. There is that stage of denial. Initially, you may struggle to accept that the relationship is truly over. You may find yourself hoping for reconciliation or believing the breakup is temporary. You're so used to the off and on and back and forth that a part of you may think the end is part of the cycle you were once trapped in.

After that, you may become angry. As the reality of the breakup sets in, you may experience intense anger towards your ex-partner, yourself, or the circumstances that led to the end of the relationship. You may feel betrayed, resentful, or outraged.

Then there's the bargaining stage. Here, you might find yourself wheeling and dealing with your ex or even striking up deals with the universe to undo the breakup or ease the heartbreak. You might start making promises or negotiating for just one more shot.

Next up is the depression stage. As the reality of the breakup hits you like a ton of bricks, you might feel intense sadness, loneliness, and despair. You might become a hermit, lose interest in things you used to love, and struggle to find meaning in your life.

Eventually, you hit the acceptance stage. Slowly but surely, you start to get used to the idea of life without your N-word. The reality of the situation starts to settle in. There's a quiet resignation, a grudging acknowledgment that it's really over. It's not easy, and the pain sticks around, but there's a flicker of moving on in the distance.

Lastly, you will start to feel hopeful. In this stage, you begin to feel a sense of hope for the future and imagine a life beyond the relationship. You may explore new opportunities, reconnect with old interests, and open yourself up to the possibility of new relationships. It's not about forgetting the past or erasing the pain but about embracing the future with open arms, ready to see what lies ahead.

Embrace the freedom you've fought so hard to reclaim, savoring every step forward and celebrating each milestone, no matter how small. Your progress is a testament to your resilience and determination. Stay committed to this journey of healing and growth, reminding yourself daily that you deserve love, respect, and happiness in every corner of your life.

I've never thought of myself as weak or foolish for enduring his chaos and ignoring my intuition when it screamed at me to leave sooner. Instead, I take responsibility for my choices, acknowledging the mistakes I made and valuing the lessons they taught me. But even now, I catch myself slipping into old patterns, making excuses for him in my mind. "Shouldn't I give him grace?" I'd wonder. "It's not his fault he's like this. He didn't wake up one day and decide to be a narcissist." Or worse, "Maybe he's good at his core, just losing the battle with his own demons."

But then clarity hits like a cold splash of water. I remember how deeply unhappy I was when I was with him. I think about the weight that lifted when I left, how my life began to improve the moment I stopped trying to fix what couldn't be repaired. Going back isn't an option. It never should be. I've learned that wasting energy patching up toxic situations only drains you, especially when your goals and theirs are on opposite paths.

If you keep playing the fixer for everyone you care about, you're signing up for a lifetime of heartache and disappointment. You must define what you want, stand firm, and be willing to pivot when necessary. It's better to build your dream life from the ground up than to endlessly renovate someone else's dysfunctional mansion. Whether it's a lover, family member, or friend, toxicity is toxicity. You must summon the courage to protect your peace without an ounce of regret.

Learn to let red flags dim your interest instead of seeing them as challenges to overcome. Be the one who escapes at the first sign of trouble, not the one who stays, hoping for change. Just as you'd pull your hand away from a burning stove to avoid getting burned, walk away from harmful situations before they leave lasting scars on your heart. Don't let anyone drain the light from your soul until you're left hollow and exhausted. Guard that spark within you because once it's extinguished, it's hard to reignite.

Whatever you're willing to tolerate is exactly what you'll get. So, demand more for yourself. Expect better. And never settle for less than the happiness and respect you deserve.

Do not allow a single person to have the remote control over your life and decide whether you will be happy or sad today. Do not allow a weapon formed against you to prosper. Life is too short to let your happiness depend on how someone else treats you. You can't control what they do, but you can control what you do. You cannot be at your best when you're upset and constantly fighting battles.

Ultimately, it's about whether this relationship brings out your best or your worst, and that should be the deciding factor on whether you stay or get the hell on. You can let your pain make you or you can let it break you. Working on yourself is needed to venture on the path of acceptance and accountability. Healing is being able to self-reflect and hold yourself accountable for things you were able to control.

You will enter a never-ending cycle of misery trying to be the right woman for the wrong man and it's useless because even at your best, you will never be good enough. Stop watering dead plants and repeatedly giving CPR to dead situations. You cannot speak life into someone that is sucking the life out of you. You cannot custom-build a man using broken pieces of yourself. You will lose yourself, trying to help him find himself and his purpose. You will not have a soft life with someone that makes life hard. Stop trying to love him into a good person. Don't believe that for one second, you can be his ride or die, and he will value and appreciate your sacrifices and reward you for it. You will always be taken for granted for the things that you do and never appreciated as a result. Because sweetheart, one sided loyalty is slavery.

The more patient and tolerant you are to BS, the more BS you are going to get. You may think he will appreciate and view you as less problematic and easier to deal with, but you will be viewed as the equivalent of that welcome door mat outside the house he wipes his feet on before entering.

Any efforts you make are to be expected as opposed to being celebrated. You will never have the safe space you desire or need. And you will drain yourself, trying continuously to pour into his empty cup, which has a hole in the bottom of it.

I believe after every relationship that failed or didn't last, you need to have a lessons-learned conversation with yourself. What did you learn about yourself? What did that relationship teach you?

From my relationship with a toxic person, I learned the power of patience. I learned to value my peace. I learned not to sacrifice who I am and what makes me feel good for someone else's happiness who doesn't deserve it. Take your bad experiences and don't harp on them. Turn them into blessings and learning experiences.

The million-dollar question is, "How do you beat a narcissist?" It's simple. The answer is you win the game when you stop playing it. That is where the real victory lies. Rewrite your life story starting with the word **F.E.A.R.** I am not talking about being scared. I am speaking of **FORGIVENESS** of self, **EVOLVE** from pain, **ALIGNMENT** with purpose, and **RECLAIM** what you lost. Love yourself the way you wished they did and be your own upgrade. The peace you will gain will be worth everything you left.

CHAPTER 13:

STARTING OVER – THE NEW BIRTH

"Stay away from anyone that makes you feel like you are hard to love"

wondered how surviving such a traumatic situation would impact my chances of diving into a new relationship. I had so many questions while I was working on my healing. Would I be damaged goods? Would fear and paranoia prevent me from having a healthy relationship? Would I turn him off with my baggage and trauma? I am here to tell you that there is love, light, and peace at the end of the tunnel. But you must be patient.

As I dipped my toes back into the dating pool, flags were popping up that may have been pastel pink, that I viewed as bright red. Subtle cues became flashing neon lights. When a man would be nice to me, I was paranoid that I was being love-bombed. When he disagreed with me, my mind would revert to being gaslighted. When he didn't respond in a timely manner,

I assumed he was cheating. Opening up about myself felt like handing over the blueprint to my soul, only to fear he'd just copy and paste. When a new suitor tried to get close to me, I would push him away. When I felt myself getting close, I would ghost him. Instead of keeping things light, I found myself trauma dumping on unsuspecting dates faster than you can say "hello." I didn't do the work on me, so I was consumed with fear and paranoia that I was following down the same path of toxicity.

It didn't take long for me to realize that putting myself back on the market was like trying to sell a house that's still under construction. The last thing I needed was to drag someone into my emotional renovation project or enter a situation with baggage and expect someone to unpack it for me.

WHAT FEELS RIGHT WHEN YOU'RE HURT WILL FEEL WRONG WHEN YOU'RE WHOLE. WHAT YOU SETTLE FOR IN YOUR PAIN WON'T SATISFY YOU IN YOUR GROWTH. Skipping the healing process proved to be a total disaster. After all, rebounding from a narcissist is not the time to embrace the "get under someone new to get over someone old" mantra. After being with a narcissist, it's crucial to resist the urge to jump into a new relationship as a quick fix. You must do the work to heal, or you risk sabotaging a perfectly good situation by misinterpreting your new partner's good intentions.

The last thing you want is to carry the hurt and pain from your previous abusive situation into a new relationship, making your new partner pay for the mistakes of your past and the sins of your N-ex. Understand that you will have baggage because trauma can take a lifetime to unpack but aim for your baggage to be a manageable carry-on rather than a fleet of check-in luggage.

I found that my toxic relationship took me through all types of attachment styles. I entered this relationship with a SECURE attachment style. In a secure attachment style, Individuals feel comfortable with intimacy and independence. They trust their partners, feel confident in the relationship, and handle conflicts constructively. I rarely enter a relationship on my guard, looking for warning signs. I typically let it flow.

After being gaslighted and manipulated, I declined into an ANXIOUS attachment style. When you have an anxious attachment style, you will develop a deep desire for closeness and intimacy, often coupled with fear of abandonment and rejection. People with this attachment style frequently need affirmation from their partners about their love and commitment. You will have a heightened sensitivity to any signs of disinterest or potential rejection, which can lead to anxiety and distress.

I inadvertently progressed into a DISORGANIZED attachment style. This was caused by inconsistent and unpredictable behaviors and the emotional rollercoaster I was riding on. Individuals with this style may exhibit a mix of anxious and avoidant tendencies, leading to confusion and instability. They often struggle with trust and intimacy, and their relationships can be tumultuous. This style usually stems from trauma, resulting in a fear of abandonment combined with a fear of closeness.

I left the relationship with an AVOIDANT attachment style. After being in a toxic relationship, someone with an avoidant attachment style might become even more distant and self-reliant. They may have an even harder time trusting others and getting emotionally close. The experience of being hurt or manipulated can reinforce their desire to protect themselves by keeping their guard up and avoiding vulnerability in future relationships.

My goal was to get back to my old self with a secure attachment style. This process took me approximately one year.

I remember speaking with someone who sought my advice on her relationship with a narcissist. She mentioned feeling like a magnet for narcissists, believing that's all she attracts. It's important to understand that you're not inherently a magnet for any specific type of person. Typically, it's not about what we attract, but who we are attracted to. We encounter good and bad people every day, but sometimes, the good ones get overlooked while the bad ones stand out more. It's not about attraction, it's about who we end up choosing, and what we accept and tolerate from them.

I'm sure you have good people in your life - friends, clients, coworkers. This shows that you do attract good. When there's no manipulation involved, we teach others how we want to be treated. We tolerate what we can and walk away when we're done. Don't be afraid to teach someone how you want to be loved.

Another person told me, "I am a healer, so I only attract toxic and broken people." I don't agree with this either. You cannot only attract broken people. You, yourself are attracted to broken people because you have a desire to heal, and subconsciously, you seek out people you can "fix" because healing gives you fulfillment.

Understanding this dynamic is essential for breaking free. The relationship may leave you feeling like you failed, questioning why your efforts weren't enough. But the reality is that no amount of love, patience, or fixing can fill the void inside a narcissist. That's their work, not yours. The question to ask yourself isn't, *Why do I attract toxic people?* but rather, *Why am I drawn to people who require fixing?* This shift in perspective places the focus on your own healing rather than theirs.

Healing this pattern begins with acknowledging your worth independent of anyone else's needs or approval. True love is not about fixing someone but about mutual respect, support, and care. You deserve a relationship where love flows both ways, where you don't have to sacrifice yourself to feel valued.

By addressing your own wounds and learning to set boundaries, you can break the cycle. The attraction to narcissists will fade as you heal, replaced by a desire for relationships that uplift and nourish you. Remember, the most important person to heal is yourself. When you do that, you'll no longer seek validation in places that harm you, you'll find it within.

Starting over after an emotionally abusive relationship can be a daunting yet empowering journey. If you're contemplating entering a new relationship, it's essential to approach this new chapter with self-awareness, care, and resilience. Here's some advice to help you navigate this transition.

First, give yourself time to heal. Healing from emotional abuse takes time, and it's crucial to give yourself the space to recover fully. Rushing into a new relationship before you're ready can lead to repeating past patterns or projecting unresolved issues onto your new partner.

Next, understand and acknowledge your experience. Recognize the impact of the emotional abuse you endured. Understanding how it affects your thoughts, behaviors, and feelings is essential for moving forward. Acknowledge your strength and resilience in surviving the abuse and use this understanding as a foundation for growth.

Rebuilding your self-esteem is also vital. Abusive relationships often erode self-esteem. Focus on activities and practices that help rebuild your confidence and sense of self-worth. Surround yourself with positive influences and engage in hobbies, work, or volunteer activities that make you feel valued and competent. Change your hair, buy some new heels, get a makeover, and hire a trainer. Do something that makes you feel good about yourself.

Trust your intuition. Your intuition is a powerful guide. If something feels off in a new relationship, trust your gut feelings. Reflect on past red flags you might have ignored and be vigilant in recognizing any similar patterns. Your intuition can help you make safer and healthier choices. Recognizing and addressing red flags in a new relationship after experiencing toxicity in a past one is crucial for safeguarding your emotional well-being and preventing the recurrence of harmful patterns. Trust your instincts and be attentive to any discomfort you may feel.

Look for consistent patterns of behavior that remind you of your previous toxic relationship, such as manipulation, control, or disrespect, and note any actions or words that make you feel uneasy. Pay attention to how your boundaries are respected and communicate openly with your partner about your concerns.

Understand what you want in a partner and a relationship. Take the time to understand what you truly want. Clarify your values, needs, and goals. Knowing what you seek will help you recognize when you find it and avoid settling for less.

Another important factor is to acknowledge the emotional baggage you're carrying. Recognize the impact of your past relationships on your feelings, thoughts, and behaviors. Denying or suppressing these experiences can lead to unresolved issues that may resurface later. Take time to reflect on your past relationship. What went wrong? What did you learn about yourself and your needs? Understanding these aspects can help you avoid repeating the same mistakes and make more informed decisions in your new relationship.

Openly communicate with your partner when you feel safe. Honest communication is crucial. When you start a new relationship, be open about your past experiences and the emotional baggage you carry. This doesn't mean unloading all your issues at once and trauma-dumping on the first date, but rather, sharing important aspects as the relationship develops. This builds trust and understanding between you and your new partner.

Establish clear boundaries based on what you've learned from your past relationship. Boundaries are essential for maintaining your emotional well-being and ensuring that your new relationship is healthy and respectful. Don't give wifey treatment when he has a girlfriend subscription.

Take it slow. There's no rush to build a new relationship. Take things slow and allow yourself to get comfortable with the new dynamics. Take things at a pace that feels comfortable for you. Allow yourself to enjoy the process of getting to know someone new without the pressure of immediate commitment.

Be patient with yourself. Understand that healing takes time, and it's okay to have setbacks. Allow the process to unfold naturally. Every step forward, no matter how small, is progress.

Be sure to embrace vulnerability and not run from it. Being vulnerable in a new relationship can be scary, especially if you've been hurt before. However, vulnerability is also a strength that fosters deeper connections.

Become open and honest about your feelings and focus on the present and the now. While learning from the past is important, try not to let it dominate your present. Focus on the positive aspects of your new relationship and its potential. Appreciate the person you're with now for who they are, rather than comparing them to your past. Don't be afraid to walk away if the situation is not serving you so you can prioritize your emotional well-being.

Starting over after an emotionally abusive relationship is challenging, but with patience, self-awareness, and support, you can create a new chapter filled with love, respect, and happiness. Embrace this journey as an opportunity to rediscover yourself and build the life and relationship you truly deserve. Trust in your worth and value as a person, and don't settle for less than you deserve in a relationship.

Stepping into a new relationship after emerging from the shadows of a toxic past requires courage and reflection. It means not just a fresh start but a sincere act of self-rediscovery and resilience. Remember, the healing journey is not a straight path. It's filled with twists, turns, and moments of growth. Allow yourself the grace and compassion to navigate through this process at your own pace, with the goal of reclaiming your sense of self and embracing the love you truly deserve.

Stay mindful to prioritize your well-being above all else. Embrace the opportunity to rewrite your narrative and redefine what love means to you. Release the weight of past traumas and allow yourself to dream, hope, and believe in the infinite possibilities. Trust in your strength, trust in your capacity to love and be loved authentically, and trust that the universe has a beautiful plan in store for you. With each new day, comes a fresh opportunity to cultivate joy, connections, and fulfillment in your life.

After you've mastered the art of spotting a narcissist and learned to love and forgive yourself, the question becomes: how do you make sure it never happens again? First, let's talk about boundaries—the ones you set, communicate, and enforce. Don't just talk about them, live them. Strengthen that backbone that was once bent or broken. Remember, narcissists loathe boundaries. They'd rather flee to find their next victim than play by your rules.

You don't have to be a "yes" woman. Saying "no" is a powerful weapon. Don't be too quick to bend, and don't mistake being agreeable for being valuable. Your world should never revolve around a man. In fact, it's the mindset that you're willing to mold yourself around him that gets you targeted in the first place. But understand that, you can shift this mentality without losing who you are.

Trust me, a man will know within minutes whether you value yourself or not. And once he knows you don't, you might as well wear a flashing neon sign that says, "easy prey." A narcissist will see you as fresh supply, and an average jerk will see a chance to exploit you. The way you carry yourself, the way you speak about yourself is the blueprint a man will follow when deciding how to treat you.

You must adopt an attitude that screams, "I am the prize." You're not afraid to walk away. You're not afraid to be single. Don't give off the slightest whiff of emotional dependence because, let's face it, A LOT OF WOMEN SEEK FROM A MAN WHAT THEY NEED TO GIVE THEMSELVES. And whatever you do, don't parade around your past trauma like a badge of honor. Telling a man how much you endured in your last relationship doesn't make you a ride-or-die, it makes you look like a vulnerable target. A man who's out to play games will spot that vulnerability and take full advantage, treating you like a sucker and indulging one lick at a time.

Learn to say "no" without feeling guilty and never drop everything to see him on short notice, jumping through fire covered hoops with gasoline thongs on. If he's only available when it suits him, politely let him know you're busy, but offer an alternative time. Being too available translates to desperation, and nothing kills attraction quicker than that. Keep control of your schedule, always. Slow things down, even when he's pushing to speed them up. The second you surrender to his last-minute whims, is the second the wrong kind of guy tightens his grip on the puppet strings.

Be selective on what you discuss and what you want from a man. Keep the blueprint to yourself. Handing a man the blueprint is like giving a thief the keys to your house and wondering why you got robbed. Don't spill all your secrets, fears, and past heartbreaks upfront, it's not therapy. It's dating! When you tell him exactly how you've been hurt and what you're looking for, you give him a cheat sheet to act the part until he's hooked you. Instead, let him show you who he really is through his actions, not through the lines you've fed him. Keep some mystery, maintain your standards, and watch how fast the wrong ones fall off when they can't crack the code. And never, never, overextend yourself trying to meet his criteria or do "wife duties" when you're barely his girlfriend. Save your energy for someone who's willing to match your energy and efforts.

You set the standard for how you are treated. You teach people how to treat you. The minute you tolerate disrespect you are teaching that person it is okay to devalue you and signal to them that your worth is negotiable. When you settle for the bare minimum, you are telling them not to prioritize you and your needs aren't important. When you refuse to accept their help, you convey your struggles aren't worth consideration. The dynamics of your relationship is a direct reflection of the standards you set and what you tolerate. It's time to raise the bar.

Don't deny yourself the beginning of a new adventure, one filled with promise and belief in your own worthiness. There is a lid for every pot. As you continue this journey, may you carry with you the lessons learned, the scars healed, and the newfound courage to embrace love in its purest form. Your future is bright, and the love that awaits you is nothing short of amazing. So, carefully take a leap of faith, trust in the process of new beginnings, and let your heart lead the way toward a love that sets your desire for yourself.

CALL TO ACTION: RECLAIM YOUR POWER

You've read my story, and now it's time to take back control of your life. This is your moment to reclaim your power, rewrite your narrative, and create a future filled with peace, purpose, and authenticity.

Make a Commitment to Yourself:

♡ I will not settle for less than I deserve.

♡ I will prioritize my emotional and mental well-being.

♡ I will set and enforce boundaries that protect my energy.

♡ I will embrace the freedom that comes from saying no.

Your First Steps Toward Empowerment:

1. **Identify one area where you need stronger boundaries.** Write it down and create a plan to act on it.
2. **Practice saying no in a safe situation.** Start small, such as declining an invitation or turning down a request that doesn't serve you.
3. **Daily Affirmations.** Repeat them daily until they become part of your mindset.
4. **Reach out for support.** Whether it's a trusted friend, a therapist, or a support group, surround yourself with people who uplift and empower you.

Daily Affirmations for Rebuilding Confidence:

♡ "I am enough as I am."

♡ "I have the right to say no without guilt."

♡ "I release the pain of my past and welcome peace into my life."

♡ "I choose relationships that nourish and uplift me."

♡ "My boundaries are a reflection of my self-respect."

♡ "I am worthy of love, kindness, and understanding."

♡ "I will no longer allow toxic people to dictate my happiness."

♡ "I have the strength to walk away from what no longer serves me."

♡ "I deserve peace, joy, and authentic connections."

♡ "I trust myself to make choices that protect my well-being."

Avoiding Toxic Situations and Narcissists:

♡ **Listen to Your Intuition:** If something feels off, trust your instincts. Narcissists often create subtle discomfort before their manipulation becomes apparent.

♡ **Educate Yourself:** Learn the red flags of toxic behavior—gaslighting, love-bombing, and excessive control are key indicators.

♡ **Establish Boundaries Early:** Be clear about your limits from the beginning of any relationship. Narcissists often test boundaries to find vulnerabilities.

♡ **Limit Contact with Known Toxic Individuals:** When possible, go low-contact or no-contact with people who consistently disrespect your boundaries.

♡ **Maintain a Support Network:** Surround yourself with people who respect and value you. They can provide perspective and strength when you encounter toxic situations.

A FINAL MESSAGE OF HOPE:

You've survived the darkness of manipulation, and now it's time to step into the daylight of freedom. Every boundary you set, every NO you speak, and every moment of self-respect brings you closer to the life you deserve. Avoiding toxic individuals is not about fear. It's about valuing yourself enough to choose peace and positivity.

The light is waiting, step boldly into it. Shine babe, shine!

ABOUT THE AUTHOR

Devyne Blessings is a writer, advocate, and businesswoman based in Atlanta, GA. Her self-help memoir, *Narcissist The Other N-Word*, is a powerful exploration of her personal journey through a toxic relationship with a covert narcissist. With raw honesty and heartfelt guidance, she inspires readers to heal, rediscover their worth, and embrace new beginnings.

Recognized with multiple humanitarian awards, Devyne's commitment to uplifting others extends beyond her writing. As a former fan-favorite on a national reality television show, she uses her platform to raise awareness about emotional resilience and the power of transformation. She also counsels individuals in toxic relationships, helping them break free and build lives rooted in confidence and self-love.

Devyne's passion for connection and creativity fuels her pursuits outside of work. Whether capturing moments through photography, traveling, and selling real estate, she finds inspiration in the beauty of everyday life. Her journey stands as a testament to the strength it takes to overcome life's challenges and transform pain into purpose.

www.ingramcontent.com/pod-product-compliance
Lightning Source LLC
Chambersburg PA
CBHW051524120626
46551CB00012B/1069